The Abingdon Waterturnpike Murder

-+->-<+-

A True-life Tale of Crime and Punishment

-+->-<+-

MARK DAVIES

Oxford Towpath Press
2003

© Mark Davies 2003
Reprinted with amendments 2008

ISBN 0 9535593 2 7

A catalogue record for this book is available from the British Library.

Published by Oxford Towpath Press,
c/o Mark Davies, 12 Hythe Bridge Arm, Oxford Canal,
Oxford OX1 2TA (tel, 01865 798254)
Towpathpress@btopenworld.com

Designed by Bryony Newhouse

Printed by Information Press, Oxford

Image on title page from 'Calendar of Prisoners', 1778–1884
(*Copyright: Oxfordshire Record Office*)

Contents

Preface

-+>-<+-

This is a true story. All the main characters in it actually lived in or near Abingdon at the end of the eighteenth century; most – ordinary working people of little note – would no doubt be greatly surprised to find themselves remembered over 200 years later. But that, I hope, is a part of the charm of this tale. Dramatic in its own right – what murder isn't, after all? – it also provides a glimpse of the realities of daily life for the labouring poor, and with it, while not excusing their actions, an understanding of why just so many such people were tempted to stray on the wrong side of the law despite the harsh deterrents. From the starting point of one robbery and murder emerges a well-organised and wide-ranging network of criminal behaviour comprising pilferage, burglary, poaching, horse-theft, and even another murder.

Essentially the story is contained within 25 documents held at the Oxfordshire Record Office in Oxford (Wi/VI/iv). These are a mixture of depositions, letters, notes, and bills retained by Christopher Willoughby, the Oxfordshire magistrate responsible for the murder enquiry. Some are undated, and the evidence may therefore have unfolded in a slightly different sequence from that described. And much relevant evidence is missing completely. Only two sworn confessions survive, for instance: those of Richard Kilby and Thomas 'Oxford Tom' Smith, men who told all in attempts – one successful, one not – to save their lives. The evidence is therefore inevitably biased in the absence of any depositions by the three other men principally involved: Charles Evans Shury, John Castle, and Giles Freeman Covington. Contemporary newspapers and other printed materials provide a little balance – but only a little. Although they were obliged inevitably to follow the official line, there is nonetheless no disguising the reporters' grudging admiration for men able to face the ultimate consequence of public execution with dignity and fortitude. From such a small stock of primary information, many assumptions have necessarily been made. Strictly speaking, therefore, words like 'probably', 'might', and 'seem' ought to appear in the text more often than they do, but they have been avoided in the interests of easier comprehension.

The two relevant newspapers of the time were *Jackson's Oxford Journal* and the *Reading Mercury and Oxford Gazette*. They often printed identical reports, but occasionally too revealed their own 'scoops', due mainly to the simple fact of their different publication days: Saturday for *Jackson's*, Monday for the *Gazette* (to use the abbreviations employed in the text). And 48 hours made a significant difference on occasions: whether it was due to skilled investigative journalism or judicious connivance by the authorities, both newspapers took only a day or two to publicise many of the developments. This was most noticeable when the victim's body was first discovered, and later when the culprits were apprehended. Strict accuracy was no doubt sacrificed for speed, and it is for the reader to judge, then as now, just how much credence to give the black and white statements of the journalistic profession! It is also worth noting that while *Jackson's* for the period has been meticulously indexed, the *Gazette* has not. Some of the Reading paper's coverage may therefore remain as yet undiscovered. One other interesting contemporary source was a single-page news sheet giving an account of Covington's execution and providing some background to the arrest which the papers had missed. In quoted text from all sources, the initial capitals used on all nouns have been edited down.

From these two main narrative sources – Willoughby's papers and the press – emerge not just one version of the death of an unremarkable working man (for history is always only ever one person's version of events!), but incidental references to many aspects of the eighteenth century which bring the context of the tale more vividly to life. The traditional annual fair of an historic market town is a colourful starting point. From there we are given a flavour of the excitement of a nationally acclaimed prize-fight, of the perilous lives and social cohesion of the Thames boatmen and the public houses they frequented, the contrasting lifestyles and concerns of the landed gentry, the demands of the Militia, the calculated risk of horse-thieving and other felonies, the nature of prisons and gruesome allure of public executions, the lawless nature of east London suburbs, and the peculiar regime of the 'wooden world' of the Royal Navy. The study of local history is full of surprises; I did not expect them to range quite so far from an ill-defined ditch containing such a little-known corpse!

Only rarely were the ages and family circumstances of individuals revealed through the sources above. To define these, it was often parish church records which provided the clues. As anyone who has attempted any genealogical studies knows, these need to be treated with some caution. Was the information recorded correctly in the first instance? Were the transcriptions accurate? What was contained in missing pages? Which individual, at a time when the stock of Christian names was relatively small and when fathers and sons often shared the same name, is being referred to? So the dates attributed to some individuals in the Appendix, while likely to be accurate, may also, in some cases, be misleadingly wrong. It was unnecessary to the thrust of the tale to include details of all these incidental characters, but the information may prove of interest to any subsequent students of this case, and indeed, anyone investigating the relevant family histories. Those people, places, and events which are covered in the Appendices printed in bold on their first relevant appearance in the main text. Some repetition of detail is inevitable; I hope it is also desirable, as a means of making both the text and the Appendices comprehensible even in isolation. It is fortunate that several of the central figures had unusual surnames – and two of them, Covington and Shury, distinctive middle names as well. About these two in particular, and their influential relatives, more can be told with certainty. Yet even then, there are two very different ways to assess both. Was Shury a ruthless criminal mastermind, or an incompetent, drunken buffoon? Was Covington a gullible but essentially well-meaning youth, or a rebellious, short-tempered bully? From the available evidence I have chosen to believe the former in both cases; I could, in both cases, be quite wrong! But then, opinions at the time – at least in respect of Covington – were evidently equally divided.

Other original sources include the accounts and minute books of Abingdon Borough Council; Assizes Records (ASSI/5/110 & 111) and Admiralty (ADM/36/10923 & ADM/52/2373 & 2384) Records held at the Public Record Office in Kew; and Quarter Sessions records, rating lists, electoral rolls, and other miscellanea held at the Berkshire Record Office in Reading, the Oxfordshire Record Office in Oxford, and the Bodleian Library in Oxford. Other essential information was obtained from the Centre for Oxfordshire Studies in Oxford, and the National Maritime Museum at Greenwich.

ACKNOWLEDGEMENTS

My principal thanks must go to Carl Boardman, the Oxfordshire County Archivist. It was his book *Oxfordshire Sinners and Villains* which first led me from an initial interest in Daniel Harris, the Oxford Prison Governor who involved himself so emphatically in the waterway history of Oxford, to look in detail at one of the most intriguing and controversial cases he was ever likely to know. General thanks are due to the ever-helpful staff of the Oxfordshire Record Office, the Centre for Oxfordshire Studies, and the Modern Papers Room at the Bodleian Library. Specific thanks are due to Nic ap Glyn, Ruth Jolly, John Lange, Jeanne McCormick, Jackie Smith, Magna Gallery (Oxford), and especially Catherine Robinson, for her immaculate (prior to my final changes!) editing and numerous suggestions.

Mark Davies
Oxford, September 2003

PLAN OF CENTRAL ABINGDON

showing streets mentioned in the text

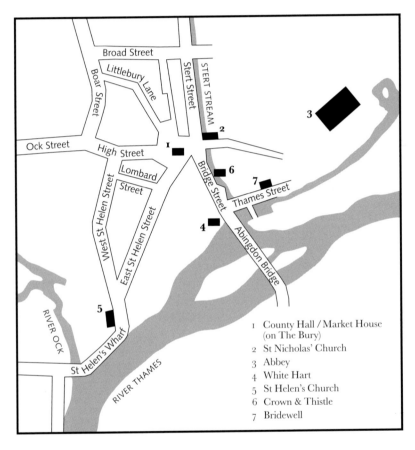

Broad Street
Littlebury Lane
Boat Street
Stert Street
STERT STREAM
Ock Street
High Street
Lombard Street
Bridge Street
Thames Street
West St Helen Street
East St Helen Street
Abingdon Bridge
RIVER OCK
St Helen's Wharf
RIVER THAMES

1   County Hall / Market House
     (on The Bury)
2   St Nicholas' Church
3   Abbey
4   White Hart
5   St Helen's Church
6   Crown & Thistle
7   Bridewell

250 YARDS

(approximate scale)

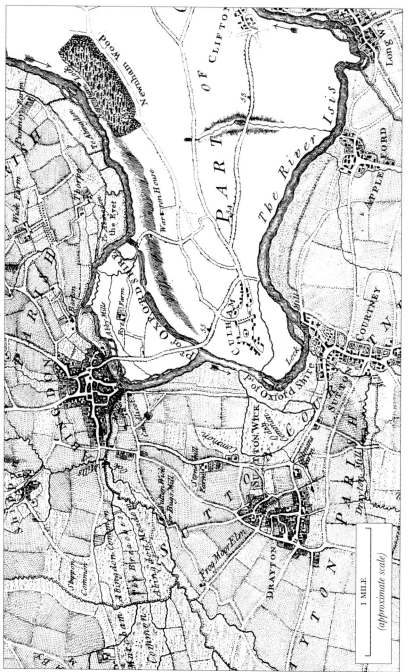

Extract from John Rocque's map of the county of Berkshire published in 1761.

I MILE

(approximate scale)

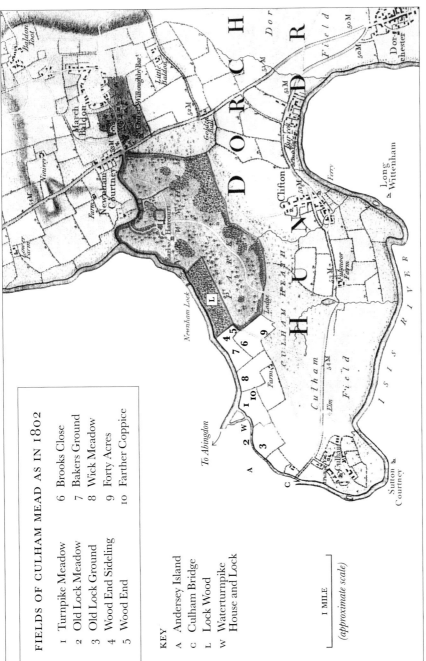

FIELDS OF CULHAM MEAD AS IN 1802

1 Turnpike Meadow
2 Old Lock Meadow
3 Old Lock Ground
4 Wood End Sideling
5 Wood End

6 Brooks Close
7 Bakers Ground
8 Wick Meadow
9 Forty Acres
10 Farther Coppice

KEY

A Andersey Island
C Culham Bridge
L Lock Wood
W Waterturnpike
    House and Lock

1 MILE
(approximate scale)

Extract from Richard Davis' map of the county of Oxfordshire published in 1797.
The 1802 map is held at the Oxfordshire Record Office: MISC CHIII/1.

⇥ Introduction ⇤

Early on the evening of Monday 8 October 1787, a linen draper called David Charteris set off from **Abingdon**'s annual **Michaelmas Fair** to walk to his home in the Oxfordshire village of Toot Baldon. He never arrived. Three days later his body was discovered in a ditch near the River Thames on the edge of the estate of Lord Harcourt of Nuneham Courtney (or Courtenay, as it is spelled today). The Coroner, noting 'many marks of violence found on the head of him', concluded that Charteris had been murdered.

And there the explanation of the death of an unremarkable local pedlar might have rested, as one of many unresolved examples of the inadequate and amateur policing of the period. There was little more the authorities could do in the absence of any witnesses, and it took another two and a half years before a series of interconnected revelations revived interest in the case, and memories were strangely refreshed. And it was not just the murder which came to light, but a whole range of other unsolved crimes going back many years.

Four principal suspects emerged. Charles Evans Shury, 42, a sometime publican from a prominent Abingdon family, and John Castle, 31, a Thames bargeman, were hanged for the murder in July 1790. A third man, Giles Freeman Covington, also from a respectable Abingdon family, followed them to the gallows in March 1791, aged 23. Which of them, if any, actually struck the fatal blow will never be known, because all three men were condemned entirely on the evidence of their accomplice, Richard Kilby, who was in his mid-twenties. All four were at the very least accessories to the crime, but much of the evidence is sufficiently ambiguous to raise considerable doubts about the relative extent of each man's guilt.

No positive identifications were ever made, even though many people were in the vicinity at the time, and Covington in particular was of a very distinctive physique. There was the mystery of a possible fifth accomplice, a woman never called in evidence, yet whose supposed exact words spoken at the moment of the pedlar's death have come down to us over time. There was also the puzzle of another suspect who lied, twice, about his whereabouts on the evening in question. And why was Charteris carrying on him the astonishingly large sum of forty guineas? What was the unspoken secret which united all the men in their dying moments? And was there a conspiracy? The authorities certainly went to extreme lengths to secure the convictions, and to influence public opinion. Covington, who had delayed capture by joining the Navy, suffered particular 'trial by media' in his absence, and stood no chance of altering opinions at his real trial. Yet many at the time considered Covington to be a wronged man, obliging the Governor of the Castle Prison in Oxford to place a reassuring paragraph in the local press. And finally, was an extraordinary letter shedding new light on his case ignored, or was it simply too late to be of influence?

All the men protested their innocence to the last. Uniquely, Covington's protestations – touching and credible – survive in the form of two letters, albeit written in oddly different styles. Of the four, Covington's case is the most intriguing. His tender age, relatively good character, ill-fated romance, and dramatic flight are guaranteed to inspire the greatest sympathy, and although his life was a short one, through his letters his name lives on.

And Covington lives on physically too, in a sense. After their executions, all three men's bodies were used for anatomical research. By some quirk of fate, Covington's skeleton has survived, and from a glass case in the Museum of Oxford it reminds thousands of visitors each year of the doubtful extent of his guilt.

'Being moved and seduced by the instigation of the Devil'

➤➤ OCTOBER 1787 ◄◄

The documentary evidence concerning the crime begins with the Coroner's inquest, or 'inquisition' as it was then called. It was held in the village of **Nuneham Courtney** on Thursday 11th October 1787, the same day the body was discovered, and three days after **David Charteris** had last been seen. The Oxfordshire Coroner **William Johnson** concluded that:

> David Chartres was found dead in a certain field in the parish of Nune-
> ham Courtnay ... and as there were many marks of violence found on
> the head of him ... the jury ... do say that he ... was by some evil dis-
> posed person or persons unknown, not having the fear of God before
> their eyes, but being moved and seduced by the instigation of the Devil
> ... wilfully and feloniously killed and murdered.

The practice of the time was to assemble a jury of twelve men as soon as the Coroner arrived. One of the jurymen was **Thomas Jackson**, who had discovered the body. Much later (at the trial of Shury and Castle in July 1790) Jackson would testify (according to *Jackson's Oxford Journal*) that

> on missing the deceased for some days, he, with others, were in search,
> it being supposed some accident must have befallen him, when they at
> length discovered the body in a sitting position in a dry ditch about six
> yards from the stile where it appeared he had received the blows, from
> some blood being then discovered; and upon taking off his hat and wig,
> the skull was laid bare in different directions, and a considerable quan-
> tity of congealed blood fell from them, and his breeches pockets were
> turned inside out.

The archive evidence does not specify who conducted the initial enquiries into the murder. Perhaps it was a parish **constable**, perhaps the keeper of the Abingdon Bridewell,[1] perhaps the Coroner William Johnson himself. Whoever he was, he added some further details after visiting the murder scene, concluding that Charteris

> was knocked down on the stile – as stile was bloody and the ground was bloody where he lay and the ditch was about two yards from the stile where he was found – at least five wounds on the head and supposed to have been giv'n by a hedge stake – skull not fractured. No money in his pocket, tho' he was seen to have money in Abingdon and at the Public Ho. His pocket seemed partly turned out.

Whether the body was six or two yards from the stile is irrelevant – although in view of the length of time it took for anyone to detect the body, the greater distance seems the more likely. With the identification of a hedge stake as the likely murder weapon, ensuing enquiries showed a particular interest in anybody known to have had a stick or cane with them at the Fair on the day in question. And the motive for the crime was clear too: Charteris had been killed for his money.

The 'horrid deed' is publicised
➤➤ OCTOBER 1787 ◄◄

The authorities were swift to publicise the crime, and the following account appeared in *Jackson's* of 13 October (and then also the *Reading Mercury and Oxford Gazette*) only two days after the body was discovered:

> Last Thursday morning David Chartres, a Scotch pedlar of Toote Balden, in this County, was found murdered in a ditch, near Lord

---

1 A prison for petty offenders.

A MURDER and ROBBERY

Oxfordſhire, 14th October, 1787.

WHEREAS a moſt inhuman Murder was on Monday Night laſt committed at Nuneham, in this County, by ſome Perſon or Perſons at preſent unknown, upon the Body of DAVID CHARTRES, a Scotch Pedlar, of Toote Balden, whoſe Head appeared to have been mortally wounded by a Hedge Stake, or ſome ſuch blunt Weapon ; this Pockets were alſo turned inſide out, and he was totally ſtripped of his Money.

This Notice is therefore given,

That whoever ſhall diſcover the Offender or Offenders, ſo that he or they may be brought to juſtice, ſhall, upon his or their Conviction, receive a Reward of TEN GUINEAS, over and above what is allowed by Act of Parliament, which Reward Chriſtopher Willoughby, Eſq. will take Care ſhall be duly paid.

Post-dated notice from *Jackson's Oxford Journal* of 13 October 1787.

Harcourt's Park, at Nuneham, with his head cut in a most shocking manner. He had been to Abingdon Fair on Monday, and in his way home stopped and drank at a Publick House near the place where he was murdered, and is supposed to have been followed from thence by some person in the House at the same time, and who committed the horrid deed.

As an itinerant salesman, Charteris was probably reasonably well known in the locality, especially if he really was from Scotland. His surname certainly has Scottish undertones, but the term '**Scotchman**' was also used generically to denote a travelling pedlar, and this might initially have misled the reporter. Certainly in all the subsequent documentation, Charteris is always called a 'Scotchman', not a Scotsman. Whatever, his was the death of a man of relatively little social importance. At a time of minimal law enforcement, many such crimes inevitably went unsolved. But the fact of the murder occurring on the very edge of the estate of a member of the aristocracy added considerable notoriety. There was a particular onus on the authorities to show their mettle. This was a time of severe rural deprivation, and cash rewards were often the best way to loosen tongues otherwise likely to remain loyally silent about the aberrations of friends or neighbours. Consequently the Oxfordshire magistrate **Christopher Willoughby** immediately offered a reward of ten guineas, over and above the forty guineas allowed by Parliament, for information resulting in a conviction. This figure was increased in subsequent weeks with a reward of twenty guineas from Willoughby's neighbour, **Lord Harcourt** himself.

So within two days of the inquest, the facts of the case were in the public domain. It says much for the efficiency and diligence of both the newspaper reporting and production of the time that the information could be so very topical. Time and again as the case developed, information would appear in print within days of its being divulged – whether with the blessing of the authorities, keen to demonstrate their successes, or through the timeless urge of journalists to sniff out a scoop, is anyone's guess!

Interrogations and alibis
⤜ OCTOBER 1787 ⤛

The **public house** mentioned by both the investigator and the newspaper was the **Waterturnpike House** of this book's title. This was one of two buildings situated near an old lock on a branch of the River Thames known as **Swift Ditch**, about a mile upstream from Abingdon. It was common for lock-keepers to supplement their income by selling **alcohol**, so the need to talk to the publican who had served Charteris was obvious. This man's name was **Thomas Hewitt**, and while it is not known what he himself had to say on the matter, three of his customers that evening emerged as the principal suspects, and were summoned for interview.

James Carter of Nuneham was known to dislike Charteris, and had 'often threatened him'. On the evening in question, Carter had been seen with his wife walking a little in front of Charteris, and was thus one of the last people to see him alive. In accounting for himself,

An artist's impression of how Swift Ditch Lock and the Waterturnpike House might have looked, depicted on an Environment Agency sign at the site in 2003.
(*Photo: Mark Davies*)

Carter reported seeing 'four persons by the waterside', an accurate observation as it later turned out, but one which was insufficient at the time to give the authorities the leads they needed.

Benjamin Woolsgrove of Toot Baldon was suspected partly because he had a 'black coloured stick' with him. He was in the clear, however, because he was able to prove that he had still been in Abingdon at the critical time, first at 'the Ship ... about five o'clock ... the Wharf for half an hour about six o'clock', then 'the Fighting Cocks', where he stayed with two friends, Henry (or Harry) Dickinson and James Baker of Nuneham, until about eight o'clock.

Robert 'Jolly Robin' Latimer of Warborough also had an alibi – in fact more than one, and they were all suspiciously contradictory! He was the only one of the three original suspects who had definitely been in the Waterturnpike House at the same time as Charteris, but he claimed to have left before Charteris did. At least that is what he told **Mrs Field**, the landlady of the public house at Burcot, when he stopped there for 'a pint or two of beer' with Benjamin Paty and his wife at about half past six. But Latimer also told Mrs Field that he had come all the way from Abingdon with the Patys, while their story was that he had caught up with them at Clifton. A third version of Latimer's movements was provided by another man who had walked back from the Fair that evening. His name was **Parker**, and the statement he made is fascinating not so much for its contradiction of Latimer's account, but for the fleeting glimpse it gives of the scene inside the all-important Waterturnpike House that evening, and of the final hour of the doomed man. As such his words, as recorded by the investigator, are worth recounting in full:

> Parker overtook Chartres about half a mile from town and about a furlong[1] from Rye Farm, about two or three acres[2] breadth before he came to a stile. They shook hands in the walk and asked each other how they did, and walked together to Water Turnpikes about 3 furlongs

1 An eighth of a mile or 220 yards
2 4840 square yards

distant. It was about half past five when they first met. He was alone and likewise Parker. Parker went into the house first and Chartres followed. They did not sit down in the house, but called for a pint of fresh beer. They found Latimer sitting down in the house by the window. They asked each other how they did and Latimer asked him to drink with him, which he refused. Latimer then sang a verse of a song, and said Chartres sung it better than any man to please him, but he declined entering into any conversation, and seemed very shy of him. They only stayed about 7 or 8 minutes. There were several people in the house and two women and a child in particular, one of which asked after some relations … Upon coming out Chartres wanted to buy his other pint as Parker had paid the first one which Parker refused as he wanted to be at home.[1] Parker came out of the house first and Chartres followed immediately.

Parker's account provides the most telling information to date, particularly in respect of the time of death. Charteris' exact age is not known, but he was referred to as 'old' in one newspaper report, and therefore presumably walked at a relatively slow pace. If Parker and he met half a mile from Abingdon at five thirty, he had probably started for home soon after five. The Waterturnpike House was another half mile. Allowing the seven or eight minutes in the pub, they must both have left it around six o'clock.

Parker's statement continued: 'they walked together, then they parted and wished each other a good night. Parker went up to Culham Common[2] and Chartres went across the Mead, and he saw him going through the meadow towards the wood, and after that time he saw him no more.' Parker arrived home (probably Dorchester) at about a quarter past seven, stopping off, like Latimer and the Patys, at Mrs Field's at Burcot on the way. Asked again about the suspect, Parker was 'very positive he left Latimer in Turnpike House', and was

1 Parker's rueful expression, when he later learned just how many pints Charteris *could* have afforded to buy him that evening, can only be imagined!
2 'Culham Heath' on Davis' map.

also helpful in determining what might have been stolen, saying that he did not believe that Charteris had a watch with him, nor did Charteris 'pull any money out of his pocket' inside the pub. A final telling comment was that 'It was quite light when he left Chartres to go along the Mead', meaning that whoever committed the crime did not have the cloak of darkness to assist them, and that anyone following Charteris across the Mead would have been clearly visible.

Despite Parker's somewhat damning counter-evidence, Latimer was obviously not the guilty man. He, like many at the Fair, had probably been drinking most of the day, and was therefore perhaps genuinely mistaken about where he had been, and with whom, and at what times!

So the Waterturnpike House had not, as originally hoped, produced the culprits from among its customers that evening. When these three main suspects – James Carter, Benjamin Woolsgrove, and Robert 'Jolly Robin' Latimer – cleared themselves, the trail went cold.

David Charteris was buried at Toot Baldon on Saturday 13 October 1787. The last public mention of him, when he was described as a linen draper, came the following January. The nature of the goods auctioned at his house in Toot Baldon on 16 January 1788 – all his 'genuine stock in trade, household furniture, and other effects' – indicate a person of reasonable affluence and no immediate heirs, or at least, none wishing to carry on his business. Otherwise, practically nothing is known about David Charteris. But then he is by no means alone in finding greater historical fame in death than in deeds.

In the short term, his death seems very rapidly to have faded out of public memory. Yet many people in Abingdon must have had their suspicions. At the end of a busy market day, the route taken by Charteris would have been used by many other pedestrians. The Fair constituted the main opportunity of the year for agricultural labourers to find new employment, so the footfall from places such as the Baldons (and Nuneham, Dorchester, Burcot, and Warborough, to name the residences of only some of the people known to have been at the Fair that day) must have been considerable. It was still light when the attack occurred, the stile was bloody, and the body was left only a few yards from the scene. Yet it took three days to find. Charteris might have been intending to walk right through Lord Harcourt's estate or alongside the River Thames, if such was tolerated, or else to skirt Lock Wood to reach the lane running towards his home village. Either way, anyone else heading in that direction seems certain to have passed over or near the fatal stile. A collective silence is apparent in the length of time it took to report the death, and in the lack of further evidence in the ensuing two years. The reason for this could be due to the reputation of one man. His name was **Charles Evans Shury**.

Charles Evans Shury
(1747–1790)
→>‑<‑

Of the four men eventually found to be complicit in the murder, Charles Evans Shury stood out. He was older than the others, and a man of reasonable standing. But he was also at the centre of a criminal network which was the bane of many a wealthy resident of Abingdon and its surrounds.

The Shurys had been present in the town since the seventeenth century, and Charles' father John, a notable brewer, had been a freeman from at least 1766. Charles' older brother, also called John, had cemented the family fortunes with favourable marriages, first to the daughter of a prominent Oxford innkeeper in 1770, and then to the daughter of a successful Oxford builder in 1777. In the meantime, the death of John Shury senior in 1771 had provided his eldest son with a further financial boost, making him one of the wealthiest residents of Abingdon before he was even thirty. There is a fair chance that Charles' subsequent criminal behaviour was due to a rebellious resentment of his elder brother's success, and that alcohol fuelled the process. The Shury family owed much of its affluence to brewing or retailing beer; the evidence suggests that Charles may have owed much of his downfall to the consumption of it!

In his early years Charles had shown little sign of criminal tendencies. Not long after his marriage in 1769 to a local girl called Martha White, he was paid by the Borough of Abingdon to look after the flood gates on the River Stert. This stream, more of a muddy ditch in the drier months, ran along the eastern side of today's Stert Street and posed a threat to some of the town's most substantial properties – including several belonging to the Shurys themselves – at times of flood. Charles held this moderately responsible position for nine years, from 1771 to 1780. It is the last indication of anything resembling conscientiousness.

What Shury did for work over the next eight years is unknown, but the first pointer to his lawless nature came in 1783, when he was fined £5 at the Reading Quarter Sessions in October 'for using a gun and beating with pointers with intent to destroy game'. It was a sign of things to come, as thefts of livestock were to be a feature of Charles Evans Shury's criminal career. Late in 1788, however, he was for the only time legitimately able to pursue this sport, being one of twenty Berkshire men, most of them from landed or urban gentry, to be awarded an annual Game Certificate. This was almost exactly a year after the Charteris murder, and a month after Shury had been awarded a licence to run an alehouse, The Chequer Inn in East St Helen's Street. It was a moment when he probably had the opportunity to go straight, and to follow his own career, albeit in the shadow of his older brother, as a minor publican. But the life of a publican, legally obliged to exhibit 'good fame, sober life and conversation', was obviously not what he was suited to. Inn-keeping was to prove his undoing, not his making, and in the autumn of 1789 The Chequer Inn became the nerve centre of a crime spree the like of which Abingdon had rarely experienced.

The details emerged only when Shury's principal sidekick, **Richard Kilby**, was arrested for the Charteris murder in May 1790. At the time, the murder investigation had drawn a complete blank, and Shury must have been encouraged to believe that if he could get away with murder, he could commit lesser offences with impunity. As indeed he did for three extraordinary weeks of the autumn of 1789 in particular. There is a touch of farce in the apparent ease with which the crimes listed by Kilby were executed. But they also illustrate a serious side to Shury: the extent of his everyday criminality, able to rely on informants in outlying villages, and willing to open his door, day or night, to receive a range of stolen goods. And receive was all he tended to do: it was others who took most of the risk, while Shury reaped the rewards, and kept the whole process nicely lubricated with alcohol in the privacy of his own licensed premises.

The quotes within the chronological version of events which follows are in Kilby's own words, and not only show Shury as the decided ringleader but introduce **John Castle** and **Giles Covington** as the other members of Shury's 'inner circle'.

'St Nicholas' Church, Abingdon' by B. Green.
The picture is dated 30 April 1782, and shows the view from the north down
Stert Street. The Stert Stream is of so little consequence that men appear
to be conversing while standing in it! The building on the left is dated 1757.
(*Copyright: Oxfordshire County Council Photographic Archive*)

Chicken broth and pigeon pie at the Chequer Inn

➤➤ OCTOBER AND NOVEMBER 1789 ◄◄

The crime spree began and ended with horse thefts. The first occurred on 24 October, and was significant in that it took Shury's criminal activities beyond the confines of Abingdon and into the realms of the London professionals, in the person of **Thomas 'Oxford Tom' Smith**. It was an association that he would live to regret.

The incident occurred when Kilby and Smith (whom Kilby appeared to know by no other name than 'Oxford Tom') met at Shury's Chequer Inn after what Kilby referred to simply as 'the Fight at Banbury'. This **Fight** had been a boxing match of national interest, attracting thousands of people from all over the country. The unorthodox, quasi-legal nature of this gathering obviously stirred rebellious thoughts. Two days after the Fight, Smith expressed his desire to steal a horse (according to Kilby's version, although Smith provided a slightly different interpretation – see page 20); Shury knew of just the thing. So the two of them set off, according to Kilby, going first to 'a house in Sutton called Dropshorts where they sell liquor without any licence, and after drinking there some short time they went up into Sutton to the churchyard there, where said Charles Evans Shury showed said Oxford Tom Mr Nichols' horse then grazing'. They then returned to The Chequer Inn, where Smith indulged in further alcoholic intake. It was dark when Kilby agreed to walk with Smith back to Sutton to steal the horse. They accomplished the deed at about half past ten, at which time Smith 'took out of his right hand coat pocket a halter which he put on Mr Nichols' cropped horse and led him out of the backside of the churchyard over a low stile'. Smith then helped Kilby to mount the horse, which he 'rode very slow until they got through Sutton'. When they encountered some flooding, they both rode on the horse as far as Abingdon Wharf, near **St Helen's Church**. From there Kilby rode through Abingdon and over the Thames while Smith retrieved his own horse from The Oxford Arms. Kilby received a guinea for his services, part of which he spent immediately on drink at Shury's inn.

On a subsequent night in October, Kilby had again been drinking at The Chequer Inn when he had chance encounters with both Giles Covington and John Castle on his way home. Kilby was either easily led, or up for any mischief going, because both men persuaded him to assist them with separate thefts within a matter of hours! It was **Benjamin Tramplett**'s White Hart Inn which Covington had his eye on. Kilby helped him to break in for a share of the five blankets and two suits which Covington threw out to him. Making a second attempt to go home to bed, with his share of Tramplett's belongings, Kilby then told how he met Castle, who asked him

> to go with him and get some fowls, and they accordingly went to the back part of Sutton towards Appleford where they entered the back part of a farm yard, and Castle pulled down some of the wall to get into the henhouse which he did and threw out to this deponent fourteen or fifteen couple of fowls which they put in a sack and brought them to the house of one Jerre Goodman, Castle's father-in-law, where they parted and each went to their respective homes to bed.

The next morning Castle took 'three couple of the fowls' to Shury. Of Henry 'Jerre' (or Cherry) **Goodman**, more will be heard later.

Next it was the turn of the hugely wealthy former MP, John Elwes of Marcham. Kilby was not involved, but nonetheless had intimate knowledge of the episode, revealing how Covington and Castle helped themselves to

> eight couple of fowls that roosted over the pig stye and not finding any more they put the fowls into a sack and returned to Abingdon and went to said Charles Evans Shury's house whom they knocked up and he came down and let them in and after that each went to their respective homes leaving all the fowls with the said Charles Evans Shury.

Subsequently, Kilby and Castle relieved Mrs Justice of Appleford of 'eight couple of fowls ... bringing them home by the waterside, they took the horse boat and went over to the Culham side and went to said Shury's house whom they knocked up to take them in, which he did, and departed to their respective homes'.

Soon afterwards, Kilby and Castle were again drinking at Shury's when he said to them, ' "My boys, I want some nice young ones (meaning fowls) for a friend," and after drinking there till eleven o'clock, said Charles Evans Shury said, "Come along boys. It is time to set out." ' By this time, no-one needed much encouragement; how easy it must have seemed, compared with horse theft and homicide! All it appeared to need was the Dutch Courage of a little alcohol. Castle and Kilby 'went as far as Jacob Jarmain's of Twopenny and from thence stole 12 young ones and seven old fowls and brought them to Shury's who got up and took them in, and said, "Well done, my boys"'.

A week later, so probably the first week of November, Shury was the recipient of more poultry, this time from a source that Castle, the bargeman, would have had more reason to know about than many: David Burgess, a boat builder near Abingdon Wharf. Chicken broth and pigeon pie must have been a real speciality of the house at The Chequer Inn during those few weeks! The gang overreached itself with the last poultry theft known to Kilby, however, and suspicions were finally aroused. Inevitably the gang gathered first at

the Chequer Inn at Abingdon when the said Charles Evans Shury proposed to rob the pidgeon house of Mr William Aldsworth of North Court ... but they waited about four or five nights for one William Pratt[1] to be of their party, but he not coming, they went to the said pidgeon house and took thereout about nine dozen and eight pidgeons which the said Charles Evans Shury sold.

---

1 The name of **William Pratt** (or Platt/Sprat) appears often in the surviving evidence, but mostly on the periphery of any serious wrongdoing.

Later, Castle would add to Kilby's list, revealing Shury as a man prepared to deal in stolen cloth as well as birds. No doubt others in Abingdon were aware that he dealt in plenty more besides! The population of Abingdon at this time was about 4,000. It seems improbable that no-one among this number would suspect Shury of some criminal involvement, but the common logic of the time was probably that the benefits of revealing a guilty person to the authorities were unlikely to be worth the potential recriminations of that person's vengeful relatives or friends. And in Shury's case, with his family's long presence in the town, the relatives were probably numerous, and the friends probably vindictive. So Abingdon remained silent on the matter, as it had about the murder two years earlier, and Shury remained confidently high-profile: clever, or devious, or possibly even popular, enough to elude detection. And ruthless enough to ensure that no-one squealed!

Eventually, however, someone did make their suspicions known. As far as can be told, the Aldsworth theft was the only time (other than the 1787 murder) that all four of the gang were simultaneously involved. For once Shury was of the party, and for once they were rumbled! Consequently, on 12 January 1790, Shury (a publican no longer, but described by then intriguingly as a 'kilnplate maker') was summoned to appear at the next Reading Quarter Sessions, to provide evidence against the other three in respect of a charge of stealing the pigeons. He was never actually required to answer to the Reading magistrates, however. A note made at the next Quarter Sessions of 13 April 1790 said simply that the requirement should be discharged 'on the motion of Mr Blackstone'.[1]

---

1 Presumably the son of the eminent Wallingford jurist, Sir William Blackstone (1723–1780).

'Abingdon Bridge', published by Samuel Ireland in 1792. The view from the east along Thames Street shows the bridge over which stolen horses were moved in one direction and stolen pigeons and chickens in the other! The spire of St Helen's dominates the scene. (*Copyright: Oxfordshire County Council Photographic Archive*)

Oxford Tom's revelations

→→ MARCH 1790 ←←

The main reason why the Reading authorities found it unnecessary to enforce the summons on Shury was that in the intervening months he had come into the frame for rather more than just a few stolen birds. The working people of Abingdon may have found it prudent to remain silent about Shury's activities, but the horse-thief Thomas 'Oxford Tom' Smith was under no such constraints.

Smith had teamed up with Shury on only two occasions. The first involved the theft of Parson Nichols' horse from Sutton, but it was a second theft, of the horse of **Simon Peck** of Rye Farm (on the track between Abingdon and the Waterturnpike House, and therefore coincidentally a place passed by Charteris and his murderers on the fatal evening), which finally brought ruin to them all. Arrested in London in December 1789, Smith was taken to Oxford on 1 March 1790, and condemned to death at the subsequent Assizes of March 4th. By statute, the execution was required to take place the following Monday. It did not, presumably because some plea-bargaining was in operation. How many condemned men in those God-fearing times, faced with the prospect of a meeting with their maker en route to eternal damnfire, would fail to tell the truth about their crimes and associates in the hope of divine mercy? Or even, if they were really fortunate, of terrestrial mercy, in the form of a pardon? For Smith it was the latter hope – albeit unrealised. **Daniel Harris**, Governor of Oxford Castle Gaol, obtained the information he required in Smith's confession of 21 March 1790, but it failed to forestall his execution the next day.

For once in this history, Kilby's (see page 15) is not the only account of a crucial event to survive. Understandably, Smith's version of the Nichols theft laid different emphasis on who instigated the mischief and who perpetrated it. According to him, Nichols had by some means given offence to Charles Shury of Abingdon, and Shury out of revenge wished the Parson's horse to be stolen, and accordingly sent to Smith for that purpose ... Shury took Smith there under a pretence of showing him how a dog would behave in the field, that Shury had to sell. But the true intent was to examine the horse, whether it was worth taking away or not. The horse was not then in the churchyard; however, the same evening Shury sent a man, a companion of his named Kilby, to see if the horse was there. If it was, Kilby was to bring it back with him. He found it and rode it out of Abingdon one mile when he delivered it into Smith's possession, for which Smith gave two guineas to Shury and one to Kilby.

The incident is indicative of Shury's vindictive nature, easily offended and prone to grudges. Flushed with the success of the Nichols theft, Shury encouraged Smith to return quickly from London for more spoil, illustrating in so doing the wide extent of his criminal knowledge and connections. Taking 'a famous horse of Mr Phillips of Culham, worth 100 guineas' would be easy, Shury thought, because he had 'a key to every door in Mr Phillips' house, as well as stables and outbuildings'. This is an impressive claim, if true, the Phillips family being the most powerful in Culham at the time. Another suggested target was 'a sporting gentleman in the neighbourhood of Abingdon, whose sister is disordered in her mind, and whose servant is very intimately acquainted with Shury, and for the bribe of five guineas would convey his master's horse to Shury to be given into the possession of Smith for which Smith was to give Shury five guineas more'.

Although only unfulfilled plans, they were incriminating of Shury nonetheless, as too was Smith's insolent footnote, apparently written in his own hand: 'Mr Shury, please to remember when you stole Lord North's gold and silver pheasants out of Bushey Park' (in Hertfordshire). It is an odd PS, suggesting that Smith wanted Shury to be under no illusions as to why he was informing on him. Had Shury perhaps cheated Smith on this occasion? The comment is suggestive of hurt feelings! And now Smith was raising the stakes. Not only

gentlemen's horses, but also game belonging to the father of a former
Prime Minister![1]

There is no record of Smith's version of the crime for which he was
actually apprehended, the theft of Simon Peck's horse from Rye Farm,
so we must once again rely on Richard Kilby for enlightenment:

> About the beginning of November last [1789] the said Charles Evans
> Shury wrote to a man who was called Oxford Tom, then in London, to
> come down, which he did and was concealed several days at the said
> Charles Evans Shury's house. And in the night of the 14th of Novem-
> ber last this deponent went with the said Oxford Tom & John Castle to
> the yard of Mr Simon Peck of Culham in the county of Oxford where
> the said Oxford Tom and John Castle went into the yard (this deponent
> standing some distance off) and thereout took a bay mare, the property
> of the said Simon Peck … The said Oxford Tom proceeded towards
> London with the mare, and the said John Castle and this deponent
> returned to Abingdon, and the next day this deponent received of the
> said John Castle half a guinea being his moiety of one guinea which he
> received of the said Oxford Tom.

The crime itself appears once again to have been relatively straightforward, but they all underestimated the determination of Peck to
retrieve his property. Many owners probably shrugged their shoulders
helplessly at the loss of their poultry, knowing that if they themselves
were not prepared to put in the effort and finance to pursue the
culprits, the authorities had insufficient means to do so for any but
the most serious or obvious felonies. The most sensible reaction to the
loss of relatively worthless stock would be not to instigate an investigation but simply to take measures to avoid any repetition. The loss of
a horse was a rather different matter, however. Simon Peck's was
worth a lot of money, and he wanted it back! As a consequence of

---

1 Lord Francis North (1704–90) was created 1st Earl of Guildford in 1752, shortly before his
son Frederick (1732–1792) became Tory MP for Banbury at the age of 22. Frederick held
this position for nearly 40 years, and was Prime Minister from 1770 to 1782.

Peck's efforts, Smith found himself behind bars, and Shury found himself drawn ever more into the authorities' sights.

Damning though Smith's revelations were, however, there was still nothing to connect Shury with murder, and even the horse-thieving was simply Smith's word against Shury's: an incorrigible London felon versus an established, if somewhat dubious, member of Abingdon society. To corroborate Smith's words, the authorities needed to locate the other man he had mentioned (and whom they had in any case already connected with the theft of Aldsworth's pigeons): Richard Kilby. Kilby, however, was not easily found, and a further two months would elapse before he would be persuaded to come clean about all his, and the others', misdemeanours.

In the meantime, further evidence was coming to light anyway, which put the thefts of horses and pigeons in a rather different context. This new information related to murder, and the source was another man already linked to the Aldsworth theft, the Thames bargeman, John Castle.

John Castle
(1759?–1790)
⟶⟩⟨⟵

It was perhaps unsurprising that certain of Shury's accomplices should start to feel nervous. 'Oxford Tom' Smith's undertaking to atone for his sins by making 'discoveries that may prove beneficial, and by giving every information in his power' had been printed in *Jackson's* a few days after his execution of 22 March 1790. Shury was too well known to flee. He would have to stay in Abingdon and try to bluff his way through the gathering storm. For anyone else associated with him or Smith, however, Abingdon was the last place they wanted to be! For Castle, escape was relatively straightforward, as the nature of his work on the barges would have taken him regularly away from Abingdon in any case. It was Spring and the river's flow would be easing to allow more boats to get on the move. In addition, this was the very beginning of a new era for the Thames, as additional traffic found its way on to the river from the new upstream canal junctions at Lechlade and Oxford. Work for experienced bargemen like Castle would be relatively plentiful at the end of a winter lull, and life was probably just beginning to look more promising. All he had to do was avoid cargoes going to Abingdon and keep his mouth shut. He succeeded only in the former.

Castle was not a native of Abingdon, but was certainly resident there by the time he was twenty, as he married an Abingdon girl, Hannah Mayo, in 1781. When she died early in 1786, it was imperative for the often-absent Castle to remarry, if only to provide care for his three young children. His choice was **Susannah Goodman** (daughter of Henry 'Cherry' Goodman, already mentioned), whom he married in December 1787, two months after the murder of Charteris. Castle may already have had a criminal record, being likely as not the John Castle convicted of stealing coal from a member of the Collins family, who were prominent Abingdon bargemasters (see Waterturnpike House in the Appendix).

If it *was* Castle, his subsequent employers must have felt he had reformed; provided he was good at his job, and there was no repetition, the incident would not necessarily have jeopardised Castle's future employment. And it is this employment, and the peculiarly self-contained nature of the boating community, which led to the downfall of the whole gang. Only in a linear, mobile community, where illiteracy made the oral tradition so strong, was an intimate conversation held on board a boat in Goring likely to travel in a matter of days through a towpath telegraph of overheard gossip and rumour to the ears of the authorities in Oxford, nearly 30 miles upstream. But it was juicy gossip indeed – what could be more so, as a topic, than murder? And it was not only the death of the Toot Baldon linen draper which was being talked about, but another of the area's suspicious deaths as well ...

Voices along the Thames
➤➤ APRIL 1790 ◄◄

Initially the authorities had only flimsy third-hand evidence to go on. The source was the most easily located section of the self-contained communities of Thames bargemen: the womenfolk, who necessarily remained in Abingdon, looking after the home or supplementing the family income with whatever work was available. From their testimonies it becomes clear that when Castle was rash enough to mention the murders to some fellow bargemen, the story rapidly found its way via the cabins of boats, busy wharves, and noisy waterside bars to reach their bankside homes – including Castle's very own! His young wife, Susannah, came to hear the story from her father, Henry 'Cherry' Goodman, who had learned the news himself from **Betsy Crawford**, the landlady of a well-established Abingdon pub, The Magpye.

Every publican, as exemplified by Mrs Field at Burcot and Thomas Hewitt at the Waterturnpike House, is a mine of local information. Betsy Crawford would have been a particularly rich vein in respect of the boating community. Both the Gleeds, her own family, and the Crawfords, into whom she had married, were boating families with widespread influence and matrimonial connections along the river.

The Magpye was probably a particularly popular choice among bargemen, therefore, as a place where men would meet to transact business and exchange news. Betsy Crawford would have been at the hub of it, the recipient of all the river rumour going! But she would also have realised the likely repercussions of this talk of murder for Abingdon's close-knit community of boatmen, whether it was true or not. Left to her own devices, she might therefore have let sleeping dogs lie, in much the same way that other Abingdon citizens seemed to have done successfully for more than two years. Betsy Crawford perhaps thought it only fair to let Castle's wife know what was being said about him, though, and asked her father to tell her. Henry Goodman was in any case a bargeman himself, and was therefore easily able to locate the men responsible for starting the rumour. At this point, it was probably still just about under control, circulating only within the confines of the immediate boating community. Castle's wife seems to have been as carelessly garrulous as her husband, however, and made the mistake of repeating the information away from the relatively safe environs of the waterside. For it was in a shop that **Susannah Spicer** overheard Susannah Castle's news, and to a townswoman it was news indeed, namely that 'three boatmen informed her father who the persons were that murdered the woman at Culham Bridge and the man at Nuneham'.

Here was not only a reference to the almost forgotten Charteris case, but, out of the blue, revelations about another murder too. It was not information that Spicer could keep to herself, and soon after the names of the three boatmen to whom Goodman had spoken were divulged. By whatever chance or effort, all three of them – Jack (John) Brown, **Will Basden**, and **Joseph Crawford** were in Abingdon on 5 April 1790, and made nearly identical statements. It says much for the seriousness with which the authorities were now taking the case that it was the magistrate Christopher Willoughby himself who came to speak to them. About a fortnight earlier (in other words, a few days after Thomas Smith's execution), according to Brown and Basden, Castle had divulged to them all that 'if he was taken and admitted on evidence that he would discover who the persons were that committed the murder at Culham Bridge and the man at Nuneham' and he 'would take a great many of them down that carried their heads very high in Abingdon'. Of the three, only Crawford mentioned any name, and it was a very familiar one, Castle having 'particularly mentioned that he could hang Charles Shury in case he should be admitted on evidence as he had done a great deal for other people'. The use of 'done' in this sentence does not, of course, imply a charitable nature, but rather the opposite, in the then accepted sense of 'doing harm'. Joseph Crawford was compromised at this point, because according to Castle's later confessions, he (and a relative, John Crawford) had been guilty of handling stolen goods. By incriminating Castle, he was in danger of highlighting his own less than blameless past dealings with the man.

This of course was all very interesting for Willoughby, but indicated no greater culpability than that Castle had been withholding information. Until he could be found, there was little more to be done – except talk to more of Castle's associates on the barges. **George Whitehead** of Sutton was one such, and took the authorities one step closer, by revealing some more familiar names. According to his statement to Christopher Willoughby on 16 April, Castle had admitted to him three weeks earlier that 'either Shury, Kilby or Covington knocked down the Scotchman and another kicked him on the head … and that they robbed him of either forty pounds or guineas'. The number of possible culprits had now grown to four, with the inclusion of Covington. The mention of a sum of money – later confirmed as forty guineas – was also new information. It was an astonishingly large amount for anyone to carry. Charteris was generally suspected of carrying cash on him, but no-one, not even Shury, could have suspected that he would have the equivalent of well over two times a typical labourer's annual income on him!

The statements of these bargemen were certainly incriminating, but not exactly *prima facie* evidence. **Peter Pickman**, an Abingdon brewer and barge owner, was a much more reliable source. Like

'St Helen's Bridge' by William Watkins Waite, from a painting owned by Christ's Hospital, Abingdon. Published in about 1815, it shows a view from some years earlier; since St Helen's Bridge over the River Ock on the left was replaced to accommodate the Wilts & Berks Canal in 1810. Peter Pickman's business premises must be among the buildings alongside St Helen's Wharf, where the barges are tied up. (*Copyright: Oxfordshire County Council Photographic Archive*)

Whitehead, he was interviewed by Christopher Willoughby on the 16th April, and like Whitehead's his recollection came from about three weeks earlier. Pickman had been writing a letter one morning at The Half Moon, a pub near the wharf from where he traded near St Helen's Church. The other interviewees had, perhaps loyally, all played down Castle's part in the affair. Pickman's words cast rather more doubt:

> Joseph Crawford of Abingdon, bargeman, came into the public house where there were several people drinking, and entered into conversation with them, and in particular with one Brown, a bargeman, and Crawford then said he heard Castle say as they were sitting down in the hatches on board the barge, that he was one of the persons that swung the woman over Culham bridge and that he had hold either of the hands or legs and that he helped throw her over the bridge and that either Kilby or Covington was with him and threw her over.

According to Pickman, Castle also 'knew who did the Scotchman, that he was present, and that after they said he was dead, a woman (who was likewise present) said Damn his blood, draw him amongst the stinging nettles'. Bizarrely, Pickman's statement concluded tamely that 'there was a great deal more conversation, the particulars of which he cannot recollect as he was busy in writing his letter.' Unless confessions to local murders were everyday subjects of conversation at The Half Moon, one can only wonder at the supreme importance of this letter!

➤➤ 'A woman who was likewise present' ◄◄

Peter Pickman was the most respectable witness yet. His firm recollection of the exact words supposed to have been spoken by the unnamed woman is intriguing. No woman was ever identified, nor mentioned again in any of the evidence. Yet it is such a precise quote, and, in view of the investigator's original observation that the 'stile was bloody and the ground was bloody' where Charteris was found, it seems a highly plausible comment. It seems unlikely that Castle would simply invent her, or that Joseph Crawford would misquote him, or that Pickman, despite his preoccupation with his all-important letter, would mishear. If there ever was a woman there, a prime candidate would have been Castle's betrothed, the loquacious Susannah Goodman. They married in the December after the murder, and her father, Henry 'Cherry' Goodman, was later shown to be complicit with some of Shury's unlawful activities. So one might say she had the criminal pedigree most likely to make her presence tolerated.

Whether or not a woman really was present, Pickman's was the most reliable evidence yet. Of the four men now brought into the frame, the prominent Shury was the most easily located, but still could not be definitively identified with any wrongdoing. Indeed, Pickman's evidence made no mention of him, and there is little doubt that a wily character like him, with influential friends and prepared alibis, would still have been difficult to pin down. All the evidence, such as it was, was still hearsay and rumour. Castle's occupation made him elusive, and Covington, the fourth man, managed to make himself still more scarce, as will be seen. So that left Kilby, the man implicated by Thomas Smith as an accomplice to at least two horse thefts instigated by Shury. Not surprisingly, Kilby too had disappeared after Smith's execution. A fixed day of reckoning was approaching, however, which would force him to break cover. May was the annual month of training for the Berkshire **Militia**, in which Kilby was, loosely speaking, a volunteer. The training began with a formal inspection in Reading on May 10th. Kilby therefore had a particular problem – either to face certain arrest by reporting tamely for duty, or be guilty of desertion by failing to show. Indeed he had another problem as well: a previous conviction.

Richard Kilby
(1764?–?)

Hardly anything is known about Kilby – his age, 26 in 1790, according to a printed Calendar of Prisoners, being a rare verifiable fact. There were several branches of the family, and as the name Richard was popular from the first appearance of Kilbys in St Helen's parish registers in 1742, it is difficult to discern exactly which Richard it is who features in this history. No doubt it is often so with informants, either wanting or assisted to disguise their true identities!

He was, however, definitely the man who was ordered in 1785 to spend three months at Abingdon's House of Correction for theft, being described at the time as a person 'of ill name and ill fame'. This earlier offence had an important bearing on subsequent events. Among the notes on the back of one of the letters sent by Daniel Harris to Willoughby was the phrase 'Kilby was before convicted'. With an existing criminal record, Kilby would have been arguably the least likely of the gang to be granted any judicial leniency, and therefore had the greatest incentive to give the authorities the information that they wanted – whether it was true or not. Who this shadowy figure really was, we may never know. When he failed to report for the Militia inspection parade in Reading, two constables were sent in search of him. These two men, Edward Bailey and Edward Webb, were paid for nine and six days respectively, at a rate of 2s a day. Eleven days after the parade, he was arrested. In the subsequent interrogation he was described as a sackweaver – an unremarkable occupation in a town renowned for its flax and hemp production, and one generally associated with the poorer sections of the community.

Kilby confesses

⤙ MAY 1790 ⤚

Kilby was located on 21 May. Presumably he was still in Berkshire, because he was taken immediately to Reading County Gaol. He was given the flogging which was a mandatory punishment for desertion from the Militia, and was interrogated the next day by the Berkshire magistrate, Henry Deane, in the presence of the Gaoler, George Knight. Also summoned at great haste were two Abingdon men with a particular interest in what Kilby had to say, Benjamin Tramplett of The White Hart Inn and Simon Peck of Rye Farm.

Kilby must have been in a vulnerable state, weakened from the flogging, and aware of his precarious situation. There was still nothing but hearsay to connect him with the murders. But Thomas Smith had implicated him in criminal acts of quite sufficient seriousness for Kilby to fear for his life, and, given his previous form, he was ideally susceptible to pressure. He did not hold back, recounting immediately the circumstances of the disappearance of Peck's horse and Aldsworth's pigeons (see pages 22 & 17) and, most crucially, as the only eye-witness account to survive, the facts of Charteris' murder, saying:

> At Abingdon Michaelmas Hiring Fair 1787 Charles Evans Shury informed this deponent, Giles Covington and John Castle that a person who was known by the name of David Charters, a travelling Scotchman, generally carried money about him, and proposed to them to go and rob him. And they accordingly set out and overtook him just at the stile within one ground of Newnham Wood. And that the said Charles Evans Shury immediately on coming up to him, knocked him down when Giles Covington also struck him. And they repeatedly followed their blows and the said Charles Evans Shury and Giles Covington stooped down and took from the said David Charters forty guineas in gold and silver, this deponent and John Castle standing by watching. And the said Charles Evans Shury, Giles Covington and this deponent

rolled the body (being then to all appearances dead) into a ditch covered with nettles and proceeded back by different ways to the house of the said Charles Evans Shury where they divided the money equally.

Mention of the nettles is an interesting detail, with echoes of the phrase which Peter Pickman attributed to the 'woman who was likewise present'. And Kilby's story is given credence by the way he acknowledged that he handled the corpse; it was an admission that he had no need to include if his motive was purely to push all the blame on to the others. His words implied that Castle was the least culpable of them all, and he made this still clearer in a second interview four days later. The issue of the murder weapon had obviously been raised again. In denying any knowledge of it, Kilby said 'at the time of meeting at said Shury's house, previous to the robbery and murder, neither he nor John Castle had any stick, nor did they mean or understand that said Charles Evans Shury and Giles Covington meant to murder the deceased'. This is all that survives of Kilby's account of the murder, although a fuller statement must have been made, akin to the much more detailed one that he would later make from the witness box.

In the days between Kilby's two confessions, Shury too had been escorted to Reading. His plan was still to bluff it out: it was only the unreliable word of a dead horse thief which incriminated him in any substantive way, after all. There were no witnesses to the murder, and Shury was undoubtedly the sort of man who had the contacts, the bravado, and the guile to wriggle out of trouble still. Unaware that Kilby had already fully implicated him, his idea was to try to pin the murder on the other two, Covington and Castle, respectively the youngest and least astute of the four of them. Whether by accident or design, his attempt to sow this idea in Kilby's mind was overheard by the Gaoler, George Knight, and recorded with persuasive accuracy in *Jackson's* record of the subsequent trial. According to Knight, 'Shury desired he would tell all he knew, to which Kilby replied, "Then I shall injure you Charles, but I suppose you want me to confess, that you may *do me.*" To this Shury replied, "*No, boy, for you shall be evidence along with me.*" ' It was a plan which might well have worked – except that for Shury, it was already too late. For it was not only Henry Deane who already possessed written evidence of Shury's guilt, but the whole county!

Speedily informed as usual, the *Gazette* printed the gist of Kilby's first confession (of 22 May) within two days. The paper also printed for the first time the names of Charles Evans Shury, Giles Covington, John Castle, and Richard Kilby as collectively guilty – although, keen as ever to cover the issues of greatest importance to their largely affluent readership, it placed as much emphasis on the theft of Tramplett's blankets, Peck's mare, and Aldsworth's pigeons as it did on the Charteris murder!

The next issue of *Jackson's* (of 29 May) put more emphasis on Shury's guilt. It also described Charteris as a 'poor honest inoffensive man' – qualities the writer is unlikely to have known about. Here is the first sign of possible media bias, with both the *Gazette* and *Jackson's* also calling the crime an 'inhuman murder'. They were certainly very quickly armed with the facts. At a time of growing criminality, and many unsolved crimes, the authorities would have been keen to publicise any success; keen too, perhaps, to steer public opinion into accepting an inevitable conviction.

Shury was taken to Oxford Castle from Reading on 29 May, Kilby on the 31st. Although they were Berkshire residents, the murder had occurred in Oxfordshire and Charteris had been a resident of that county, so that was where they would stand trial.

'View of Abingdon from Nuneham Park' published by John and Josiah Boydell in 1794.
Looking west, the view shows Culham Mead, where Charteris met his death, to the left of the Thames.
Where the river splits, the left-hand branch appears to be Swift Ditch, although the course of the other branch,
seeming to flow to the north of Abingdon, is misleading. *(Photo: Mark Davies)*

Castle is taken
→→ JUNE 1790 ←←

Castle was next to contemplate the insides of first the Reading then the Oxford Gaol. Constables were sent in search of him, furnished with this description:

> lived ... at Abingdon and there worked as a bargeman and is well known by the West Country bargemen working in the Oxford & Abingdon boats to and from London. About 5 feet 4 inches high. Fit and strong-made, his complexion fair, thin visage and light sandy hair, a stiff sandy beard, light grey eyes, pocked nose and little pitted with the smallpox; mostly wears a blue bargeman's jacket and blue breeches.

The constables also had some pointers to his whereabouts, namely that he was likely to be on a barge called the *Fortune of War*, that he 'always slept aboard the boats', and a starting point for their enquiries might be 'a public house in parish Staines on a common. Landlord's name Baker.' But Castle had already fled, realising that the boats – slow moving and obvious – were no longer a safe refuge. It was to no avail, and he was arrested in the village of Sparsholt, about three miles west of Wantage, on the Portway (an ancient east-west route running at this point parallel to the Ridgeway, but at a lower level). Abingdon was not Castle's birthplace, so, considering his familiarity with the bargemen of the West Country, perhaps it is from the west that he hailed, and was heading in this direction when apprehended. He might even have been quite relieved to see an end to his wretched existence in exile. Castle had earlier told William Basden that even if he was arrested it would be worth it, as he would at least 'then have his clothes and money'!

Like Kilby, Castle was interviewed at Reading Gaol by Henry Deane, who did not hesitate to send him on to join the others in

Oxford on June 1st. A note written to his Oxfordshire counterpart Christopher Willoughby is revealing not so much for its appraisal of Castle's attitude, but because it shows that both of them had already made up their minds about Shury. He wrote:

> Castle was brought to me quite cool this morning, but he still persists in his innocence. Colonel Powney and Mr Hodgkinson (our chaplain) were both present, and both declare they never saw a more hardened man … He depends on proving an alibi. He was acting, he says, as waiter at some public house the whole of the day and evening on which the murder was committed. He really does not seem to me as deserving the least favour but is as bad, to appearance, as Shury himself.

Once in Oxford, Castle confessed to a series of petty thefts, almost all from either a barge or a riverside property. He also named plenty of accomplices, among them Isaac Evans, William Pratt, and several bargemen, including Joseph Crawford. But Shury's was the name, once again, which dominated, showing that he had the capability to dispose of considerable quantities of cloth and hemp, as well as pigeons and chickens. The names of Kilby and Covington are conspicuously missing.

Castle and Shury had to wait over a month until the next Oxfordshire Assizes to learn their fates. In early July, they were joined in Oxford Castle by another man with reason to curse Thomas 'Oxford Tom' Smith. This was James Williams, who had helped Smith to steal a horse from his master's house in Wheatley, a village near Oxford on the main road to London. His capture had come largely as a result of the endeavours of Simon Peck, a man obviously prepared to go to some lengths on behalf of others as well as himself.

Many of the other prisoners held in Oxford Castle at that time would have assisted with the building of the new terminus of the Oxford Canal, which lay only a few hundred yards away, or with the concurrent improvements on the Thames, in both of which the Gaoler Daniel Harris was intimately involved. No doubt these innovative building works and the enhanced waterway economy were a frequent topic of conversation in the cells. How Castle must have cursed the verbal indiscretions which would deny him any opportunity to benefit!

The trial of Shury and Castle
➤➤ 14 JULY 1790 ◀◀

Castle and Shury were jointly tried by Mr Justice Buller and Mr Baron Perryn on Wednesday 14 July. The identical accounts in *Jackson's* of 17 July and the *Gazette* of 19 July 1790 referred to only five witnesses for the prosecution. Conspicuously absent were the names of those early exonerated suspects, especially James Carter, who had been 'one of the last persons to see Charteris alive', and Robert Latimer, who conversed briefly with Charteris inside the Waterturnpike House, and was apparently able to be in two places at once! Neither was Parker, a significantly material witness, called in evidence.

Among the witnesses who *were* called that day was Thomas Jackson, who had discovered the body. Another was a bargeman called **William Bossom**, who summarised many of the river community's earlier statements to assert that 'Castle had some time ago confessed to him that he had no rest, night nor day, from the horror of having been concerned in the murder of the Scotchman.' A third witness was John King, who

> was returning from Abingdon Fair to Dorchester, in company with James Patey, and observed four men at a place called Ditch End, in the second ground beyond the Water Turnpike, three of whom he deposed to be Castle, Kilby and Shury; that he saw Charteris before

them, and afterwards in crossing Culham Heath he heard a cry of distress, which seemed to come from the place where the body was afterwards found.

James Patey corroborated King's story, 'except that he could only identify the person of Castle, though he believed Shury and Kilby to have been of the party'. The personal valour of King and Patey, who heard the 'cry of distress' yet continued on their way home, might be questioned. We do not know how old they were, but in these lawless times it would take a brave soul, young or otherwise, to risk further investigation, with the autumn night approaching. What they *might* have done, however, is report their suspicions to the authorities. One can only assume that they, like many others, chose not to become involved because of Shury's reputation and their own fears of revenge. It seems odd, though, given the other possibilities, that the prosecution chose to use two witnesses who had tried to convince themselves for over two years that they had never seen or heard a thing!

Next came the fifth witness, Richard Kilby, whose testimony was the only one the prosecution really needed, the word of a man who was prepared to betray his friends in return for his life, yet who could easily have been more guilty than any of them. Along with his earlier confession, it is the only surviving version of the exact events of that evening. Almost certainly Kilby played down his own part in the affair – who wouldn't, after all? – but essentially it is probably an accurate account of how things happened, although it may have been that it was different individuals who *made* them happen!

Kilby testified that Shury had approached the three others during the afternoon of the Fair, and told them 'that he would help them to a good booty in robbing an old Scotchman on his way home'. Consequently the four of them met at Shury's house (his domestic home, that is, not The Chequer Inn, as this was before Shury became a publican). At about five o'clock Shury and Castle set off, with Kilby and Covington following about ten minutes later. The newspaper account of the trial continued:

They joined company near the Water Turnpike, but about Ditch End again separated, Kilby keeping the path, whilst Shury, Castle and Covington kept to the left towards the river, the two first witnesses at that time coming up, who went up the hill crossing Culham Heath on their way to Dorchester.

Yet neither King nor Patey (the two witnesses referred to) had identified Covington among the three, even though, as subsequent evidence would show, he was of a very distinctive physique. The four of them joined together again, and (exactly as per Kilby's earlier statement)

> as soon as Charteris had got over the stile, Shury struck him a violent blow on the head with a hedge stake, which blow was instantly followed by others from him and Covington till they judged him dead, himself and Castle being all this while a few yards distant, 'till Covington called for assistance to roll the body into the ditch.

The gang then dispersed. Kilby walked back to Abingdon with Castle, and all four reunited later at Shury's. There he divided the spoils, 'giving each of them in gold and silver ten guineas, saying *"Now, my boys, let us be true to each other"*'. It is a strange thing that the newspaper should record Shury's words as a quotation, announced as they must have been from the witness box by Kilby, who was at that precise moment being anything *but* true to his companions! Shury probably had legal representation, but if so the defence was pretty half-hearted, and based on a possibility that Kilby, on meeting the Abingdon coach in London, 'had used expressions tending to manifest a design of what is called *doing* Shury'. In other words, that it was Kilby who was the guilty party, and that once the heat was on, he had always intended bearing false witness against Shury. The prosecution, however, somehow convinced the court that this is not what Kilby said, but, somewhat bizarrely, that he was merely enquiring if any handbills had been sent to London in respect of the theft of Aldsworth's pigeons.

A guilty verdict was never in doubt. The jury's official verdict, much of it taken verbatim from the coroner's findings on the day of the inquest, found Shury guilty of striking the fatal blow

> with a certain large wooden stick of the value one penny that the said Charles Evans Shury with both his hands then and there had and held, in and upon the head of him, the said David Charteris ... giving to the said David Charteris one mortal wound of the length of three inches and of the depth of two inches.

Castle was found guilty of 'aiding, abetting, assisting, helping, comforting and maintaining' Shury in this act. So too was Covington, *in absentia*, all three 'not having the fear of God before their eyes, but being moved and seduced by the instigation of the Devil'. Kilby's name is conspicuously absent.

The judge, no doubt well-versed in the requisite terminology through much practice

> with a most awful solemnity, impressed upon the audience, as well as the prisoners, the superintending providence of the Supreme Being, in so often bringing to light the most secret transactions of this horrid complexion, by an impulse which so frequently disturbs the breast of the perpetrators; and having finally assured them that they were not to entertain the most distant hope of mercy in this world, recommended to them to make the best use of the few hours allotted to them for making their peace with God.

'The New County Jail with the old Castle Tower, Oxford' as drawn by a pupil of the Oxford artist John Malchair in 1797. In the centre is the main gate, above which executions were held within clear view of the public. The sturdy walls represent a remarkable transformation of the dilapidated scene of a few years earlier, and one of many Oxford building projects of the time in which the Prison Governor, Daniel Harris, could take some personal pride.

'The final exit of Shury and Castle'
→→ 19 JULY 1790 ←←

John Castle and Charles Evans Shury were executed together above
the main gate to Oxford Castle the following Monday morning.
Jackson's of 24 July and the *Gazette* of 26 July carried identical
accounts, reporting that:

> A prodigious concourse of people flocked ... from divers parts to
> be spectators at the final exit of Shury and Castle ... and yet many
> hundreds were disappointed, by arriving too late.
>
> They were brought out of the chapel about half past eight in the
> morning, and having ascended the tower over the gateway they
> alternately harangued the multitude, confessing to having led wicked
> and dissolute lives, which they attributed to having been corrupted
> by bad company, but both positively denied the crime for which they
> were going to suffer. They also spoke to several persons whom they
> distinguished in the crowd beneath, though they were at the elevation
> of thirty three feet from the ground, and their general behaviour
> was hardened and vindictive in the highest degree. A little before the
> execution, Castle dropped a letter, directed to William Bossom, written
> for him by one of the prisoners, the purport of which was to charge
> Bossom with having borne false testimony upon the trial; and Shury
> called to another telling him he would go out like the snuff of a candle,
> as would his whole family.

This comment says much about Shury. Threatening retribution to
the last would seem to confirm that his reputation was such that
few people would dare cross him. Whatever his true nature, one can
only admire his ability to keep a sense of humour to the end. The
'gallows speech' was expected additional entertainment, and Shury
did not disappoint. The phrase he is quoted as shouting to the crowd
– 'My Boys! God bless you. I am as innocent as a lamb of what

I am going to suffer for, so God forgive you all!' – shows all the bravado one might expect from what is known of him. Yet it could also smack of irony, the comment of one who knows full well the extent of his guilt, and is aware that most people there present were probably equally cognisant!

Immediately Castle 'seemed much agitated, whilst he was nevertheless persisting in a denial, and it is probable Shury began to be afraid his resolution should fail, and therefore called to the executioner to "turn them off or that fellow would keep talking all the day"'. This is an intriguing conclusion. Shury imbued the event with sardonic wit even to the final moments, but was his haste to terminate proceedings really due to a fear that Castle might reveal more? If it had actually all happened the way Kilby told it, showing Castle to be no more guilty than himself, it would have been utterly natural for Castle to have corroborated Kilby's story when all other hope was lost. Yet he did not, even though his oft-repeated threat to 'take a great many of them down that carried their heads very high in Abingdon' had earlier made Shury his prime target. Later evidence suggests that all of the accused were holding something back, and it was not their own guilt. Could it have been that there really had been a fifth person at the murder, the mystery woman, and that Shury feared that Castle was about to reveal her name? Or was it simply Shury's fearsome nature which made Castle hold his tongue? An ignorant man, thinking himself inescapably destined for hell, he would not have relished the idea of betraying in his last moment the ruthless, vengeful man with whom he might have to spend eternity!

Kilby is pardoned

→→ SEPTEMBER 1790 ←←

Even with Covington still at large, Richard Kilby got his pardon – very fortunately, one might think, considering that his role in the affair, by his own admission, was no less significant than Castle's. The pardon was dated 13 July – the very day before Castle and Shury's trial – and it exonerated Kilby from the only crime he had actually been sentenced for: a theft of goods and livestock in November 1784. The bill for preparing the pardon was held back until 8 September 1790, and came to a massive £88 10s 6d. Someone was evidently very determined to ensure that justice was done – or at least seen to be done – whatever the cost. But true value for money would be realised only on the arrest of culprit number four: Giles Covington.

Giles Freeman Covington

(1767–1791)

→→←←

After John Castle had been taken to Oxford on June 1st, the *Gazette* of 7 June 1790 confidently claimed:

> Giles Covington is the only remaining person of the gang that is now at large; and as considerable rewards are offered for his apprehension, there is little doubt that we shall soon hear of his being in custody. From the confession of Oxford Tom a short time before his execution, there is great reason to suspect that Covington was concerned in murdering a poor travelling woman, some time since, and throwing her body into the water, from off Culham Bridge.

The paper's confidence in an early arrest was misplaced: Covington was to prove elusive for some six months more, and no further reference was ever made to the murder of the **pauper woman**.

Giles Freeman Covington was the youngest of the gang, but unlike Castle and Kilby could not claim poverty as the motivating force of his criminal behaviour. His was a comfortable upbringing in a respectable home. He had been baptised at St Helen's on 12 April 1767, the youngest of four boys. His parents, **Roger** and Elizabeth, had moved to Abingdon from London before the birth of their eldest son in 1755. By the 1780s Roger Covington had risen to become a respected member of Abingdon society. In 1780 he was elected to the prestigious position of Bellman (sometimes called Beadle or Town Cryer). Among numerous other duties, this meant that it was Roger who was responsible for the night watch in Abingdon. One wonders what he and his employers, the Abingdon Corporation, would have made of the events of October and November 1789, months when men seemed able to move almost at will along the night-time streets of Abingdon with stolen horses and armfuls of poultry! Indeed it is possible that Giles was the very reason why they could do so. It is easy to imagine him passing on privileged information about his father's nocturnal routine, or distracting him while his friends advanced their criminal careers.

Certainly Giles showed an early tendency to rebel. His older brothers all excelled in their fields. Edward, the oldest, became a baker of particular note; John trained as a tailor, but was running a substantial pub called The Chaise and Horses by the end of the century; Thomas followed their father's trade as a very successful tailor.

Giles was not possessed of a temperament suited to such sedentary trades, having (as it was put after his death) 'an aversion to confinement'. He had an early brush with the law in 1786, being indicted, but cleared, of stealing turkeys. He would then have been 19; but, as later evidence would show, this was not the first time he had strayed the wrong side of the law.

On 5 February 1789, he married a local girl called **Ann Gilkes**, whose father, Thomas, had been a plumber and glazier – a much respected profession, but often also an unhealthy one on account of the pernicious effects of frequent exposure to lead. Possibly this is why Ann's parents were both dead by the time of the wedding. She was therefore given away by her older brother, Richard. The wedding was held at St Nicolas' Church – which is significant, in that both the Covington and Gilkes families generally worshipped at St Helen's. There was no Covington among the witnesses, suggesting that it was a marriage that Giles' parents disapproved of. With some reason perhaps, because the couple already had a one-year-old illegitimate daughter, Elizabeth. Given Roger Covington's municipal responsibilities, his youngest son must have been an exasperation to him. First the business with the turkeys, then a bastard child to contemplate, and now an unsuitable marriage. Giles was then aged 21, however, and free to marry whomever he chose. So that is what he did, in February 1789, but in the 'other' church of St Nicolas.

This was the very church where Covington was first led into criminal ways, and it was Charles Shury – who else?! – who was the cause! In August 1785 they had broken into the church together, and stolen the church silver. This was a crime probably regarded as beyond the pale even by the petty thieves with whom Shury seems to have surrounded himself. Relieving tradesmen of a little of their merchandise, or the gentry of their livestock, was one thing; sacrilege was quite another. The two of them would therefore have had an especial incentive to keep this knowledge to themselves. It was a dangerous secret – especially for the 18-year-old Covington, perhaps, who from that moment probably became fatally vulnerable to the older man's undoubted powers of persuasion.

Extract from engraving of *HMS London* 'carrying 90 guns and 850 men, off Ram Head, near Plymouth'. It is dated 4 June 1781. (*Copyright: National Maritime Museum, Greenwich*)

Covington seeks sanctuary:
London, then the *London*

➤➤ MAY 1790 ◄◄

It is not clear where Covington was when the news of Thomas 'Oxford Tom' Smith's confession broke in March 1790. Whether he fled to London on account of it, or was already there, he and the heavily pregnant Ann (and presumably their infant daughter, Elizabeth) were certainly resident in London by early May 1790. A description was issued:

> aged about 20 years, born at Abingdon, has lived there ever since, five feet nine inches high, very stout and well made, flaxen hair, pale complexion, light grey eyes, long visage, large, long nose, remarkably gruff in speech, mostly wears a blue coat with white metal buttons, white linen waistcoat, brown corduroy breeches, walks very upright, rather swaggering in his gait, supposed to be on board an Indiaman.[1]

Covington did indeed go to sea, but never got anywhere close to India! He waited until the birth of his son, also named Gyles Freeman, on 7 May 1790, but was safely afloat by the time the child was christened the following month. The church chosen was St Sepulchre's, Holborn, where a certain Roger Covington had been christened in 1729. This was no coincidence. Covington had chosen to seek refuge among relatives. The Covingtons were numerous in Holborn and Aldersgate, and the couple found sanctuary in the latter. It was probably essential. Even being 'very stout and well made' would not necessarily protect a raw youth from the provinces, plunged into a city swarming with dangers of all kinds. Covington must have realised that with his unusual physique and 'remarkably gruff' voice he could not remain undetected for long.

---

1 A ship engaged in trade with India or the Indies.

➤➤ 49 ◄◄

Joining the Navy would have presented Covington with one of his best chances of distancing himself from his past. Indeed, it probably seemed quite appealing in its own right. He was an active, strong individual, with an evident sense of adventure. He might well have envied John Castle his itinerant lifestyle, and would certainly have had exposure to the life and habits of other Thames bargemen in Abingdon. Additionally, one branch of the Covington family lived in Queenhithe, next to the Thames, and some earned a living as Thames watermen, a highly skilled job in the busy and dangerous tidal waters of Britain's premier port. So there was no doubt that Covington was well suited both by connection and disposition to a life on the ocean wave, and within a couple of days of the birth of his son, he found himself aboard one of the Navy's most prized vessels, **HMS London**. Her muster tables show that he enlisted voluntarily at Woolwich on May 11th, for a bounty of £1, and reported for duty on the 12th.

1790 was a very peaceful year by the standards of the period, as Britain attempted to recover from the damaging effects of American independence by embarking on a series of diplomatic alliances. There were still moments of international tension, however, and it was a dispute with Spain which dictated the movements and routines aboard the *London* during the first few months of Covington's service. When Spain backed down in the middle of September, the *London* headed back to Spithead, near Portsmouth. And there she remained – rather to the frustration and concern of Covington, no doubt, who might have preferred less permanent and more distant reminders of the *terra firma* on which he was such a wanted man.

At least by enlisting on such a large vessel, Covington was guaranteed a degree of anonymity. The *London* had a nominal complement of 850 men, but there were often many more than that aboard, amounting to over a thousand in October, when more than three hundred marines and Vice Admiral Sir Alexander Hood's retinue of 50 men came on board. The arrival of the marines must have been an unpleasant reminder for Covington of his proximity to land-based authority, and the implementation of naval justice, for which the entire crew would normally be assembled, must have given him regular cause for reflection. Punishments were usually for insolence, fighting, or theft, but from Covington's point of view, the most poignant sight would have been the receipt on board of a condemned man from another ship. This was on the 22nd December, and would have been a timely reminder that though the Royal Navy was known for its stubborn independence in matters of criminal misdemeanour by its sailors, it was no absolute guarantor of immunity from justice.

Whatever the reality of his behaviour in Abingdon, Covington could take some pride in his part in this demonstration of Britain's diplomatic and naval recovery. A news sheet published after his execution was correct in saying:

> On board the ship he had been so regular and attentive to his duty as to be rated an able seaman much earlier than is usual with persons who have never before been at sea, and during this single cruize seemed to have acquired a perfect knowledge of the dialect of sailors.

The pressgang was the reviled but generally accepted means of ensuring sufficient manpower to meet international maritime needs, so volunteers as adept as Covington were greatly treasured. A man left his criminal past on the landward side of the gangplank when he entered the 'wooden world' of one of his majesty's ships, and unless his behaviour compelled otherwise, that is how the Navy preferred it.

But eighteenth-century sailors did not so much join the Navy as join a ship's company. As soon as that ship's term of duty was over, the crew would be paid off and left to find alternative employment as best they could. This may have been Covington's lot at the end of the year. On 13 November 1790 *Jackson's* announced a convention terminating the differences between Spain and Britain, but added that 'notwithstanding the present pacific appearance' the enrolment bounties were to be continued until December 31st. It can surely be no coincidence that only two days after this date, Covington was arrested.

Arrest of a 'most atrocious offender'

➤➤ JANUARY 1791 ◄◄

It had always been only a matter of time. When Christopher Willoughby learned that Covington had gone to London, he advised the chief magistrate of **Bow Street, Sir Sampson Wright**. Wright's enquiries showed that Covington had gone to sea. Confident in his good relations with the Admiralty, Wright felt able to assure Willoughby that neither identifying the ship nor 'the getting of this delinquent into custody will be attended with any difficulty'.

Nor should it have been, really. Given the Navy's efficient record keeping, there appears to have been no good reason why Covington should have remained untraceable. Surprisingly for a man-on-the-run, he took little care to cover his tracks, and used his real age, birthplace, and name – or at least sufficient of the latter to represent a poor attempt at disguise. Perhaps it was it an ill-advised rush of youthful bravado which led him simply to drop the Covington and call himself Giles Freeman when registering on board in May, taunting the authorities with the literal meaning of his middle name? He was to pay for his cheek. At some point over the ensuing seven months, someone put two and two together, and, in a mysteriously anonymous way, described in *Jackson's* as 'circumstances which appear highly providential', his identity became clear.

These 'providential' circumstances were summarised in the news sheet published on the day of Covington's subsequent, inevitable, execution. They were details which only the Metropolitan authorities could have provided, revealing that eventually

> one of the Bow Street Officers, then searching about different parts of London where [Covington] was supposed to be concealed, and whilst ... all enquiries appeared fruitless, found in one of his pockets, written on a piece of paper, the name of *Giles Freeman*, on board the London. Conceiving that *Giles Covington* might possibly be the man, under the

name of *Giles Freeman*, the ship's books were searched, and Freeman found to be on board, but the London Man of War was then upon a cruize, being the Flag Ship in the Fleet of Observation. Fortunately, however, the Regulating Captain perfectly recollected his name and person, being a tall and remarkable fine figure.

'Highly providential' circumstances indeed, simply to find that some anonymous person had popped a vital clue in your pocket! And further reason to ponder the evidence of John King and James Patey, those two trial witnesses whose suspect valour led them to continue on their way home that fateful October evening in 1787, rather than investigate – or even mention to anyone – Charteris' cry of distress. If Covington had truly been among the men who followed Charteris, how was it that they failed to spot his 'tall and remarkable fine figure', yet were able to name the other three?

So on Monday 3 January 1791 a 'D' for deserted was written against the name Giles Freeman in the *London*'s muster-tables, because the previous day 'at 11 came on board the Civil Power, and demanded Giles Freeman, seaman, prisoner, and took him on shore'. The *Gazette* provided further details of both the arrest and again of Covington's distinctive physique in describing how he

> was apprehended by Jealous, one of the Bow Street officers, on board the London man of war at Spithead. He is a remarkable stout fellow, and was deemed an excellent pugilist; it was therefore necessary effec-tually to secure him, for which purpose he had an iron belt fastened about his waist, to which his arms were securely bolted, and heavy irons on both his legs.

Under these conditions, Covington was taken from Spithead to Oxford Castle on 3 January. Christopher Willoughby was made swiftly aware, and the very same day Kilby was summoned to denounce Covington in person. The months since his betrayal of his companions must have been nervous ones for Kilby. There were no doubt plenty of compromised people in Abingdon thirsting for his blood, and his pardon could never be absolute until the pugilistic Covington was behind bars. Even with official protection, which, as a vital and costly witness, he probably had, the doubts and fears must have been many over the six months that he had to wait to face Covington in person once again. Unsurprisingly he stuck to his story. While still portraying Castle to be no more guilty than himself, he avowed that 'Covington was one of the persons that robbed and murdered David Charteris a travelling Scotchman about 3 years ago at Nuneham ... and that the said Giles Covington struck David Charteris after he was knocked down by Charles Shury'.

The press had been primed, and had no intention of waiting for the trial to deliver its verdict. In its issue of 8 January, *Jackson's* was already in no doubt that Covington was 'one of the accomplices in the inhuman murder of David Charteris' and a 'most atrocious offender'.

There were two months until the next Assizes. The authorities were taking no chances, and the extreme precautions taken when transporting Covington to Oxford were maintained inside the prison too:

> Upon being delivered into custody in Oxford, due care was taken: he was never suffered to be alone, night or day, and orders were given that no visitors or others should be admitted without a written order from some magistrate of the county. The visits of his father were the chief, with those of his attorney upon the approach of the Assizes.

'The dreadful sentence of the law'

→→ 4 MARCH 1791 ←←

In contrast to the extensive coverage of the trial of Shury and Castle, Covington's was barely commented on in the press. There was never any doubt anyway. It was simply Kilby's word against Covington's, so 'when the same full and satisfactory chain of evidence was adduced on which the others had been convicted, and after a fair and patient investigation of this horrid transaction had been summed up, the jury, without the least hesitation, pronounced the prisoner *Guilty*'.

The official verdict found Covington guilty, as Castle had been, of being an accessory by 'feloniously and wilfully and of his malice aforethought being present, aiding, helping comfort and maintain Charles Evans Shury in the wilful murder of David Charteris'.

According to the newspapers, the judge then passed 'the dreadful sentence of the law in a most pathetic and animated speech addressed to the feelings of the human heart, which appeared to have far greater effect upon the court than the prisoner'. The comment seems to imply that those in attendance were surprised by the verdict, even if Covington was not. Certainly, he had been much more animated earlier in the proceedings. Indeed, 'so audacious was Covington's behaviour that during his trial, whilst Kilby was giving evidence, he made a sudden spring towards him, and attempted a blow to his head'. The point at which Covington became so indignant that he could take no more came as Kilby 'was giving evidence of the manner in which he gave Charteris the blows by which he was murdered'. The papers of a week later expanded on this animosity, saying that Covington

in an unguarded moment, with some bitter imprecations, charged Kilby with falsehood and perjury in giving testimony that any of the blows were given by him to Chartres, well knowing that he was not at that time within the length of a couple of hop poles of his person.

Before Covington was led away, he and Kilby further engaged in 'some serious expostulations' which did neither of them any credit. In the heat of the exchange, Covington acknowledged his part in a crime he had only just denied under oath, namely the recurring theft of Aldsworth's pigeons. Kilby meanwhile let slip details of his criminal past which only a select few were intended to know, acknowledging 'divers crimes which at present it would be imprudent to divulge'. Covington's outrage was understandable. Kilby's long criminal past included stealing horses, after all, whereas Covington was only ever accused of three thefts of property. Daniel Harris, writing to Christopher Willoughby on the day of Covington's subsequent execution, was also of that opinion:

> Covington persisted in his innocence to the last with respect to the murder, though he has confessed that himself and Shury stole the church plate, that Kilby and him stole Tramplet's blankets, and that he perjured himself in the affair of the pigeons – which is the substance of everything he made known and which he declared was every affair of the kind he had been concerned in.

'And the executioner did his office'

➤➤ 7 MARCH 1791 ◄◄

In accordance with statute, Covington's execution was held on the Monday after the trial. The reports in both *Jackson's* of 12 March and the *Gazette* of two days later were identical, save for one highly significant paragraph. Thomas 'Oxford Tom' Smith had used his last few moments to speak out in repentance; Shury and Castle in recrimination. If this kind of additional entertainment was expected of Covington, he disappointed. All the papers had to say was that he was executed at about a quarter to ten upon the tower at the entrance to our Castle ... in the presence of a prodigious multitude of spectators. He came upon the scaffold dressed in his sailor's jacket and trowsers, with white gloves and a white hatband, and although he had summoned up all his fortitude, he was nevertheless pale as a corpse, and exceedingly agitated. Having mounted the drop, he threw over a paper which he desired might be read aloud, yet without attempting to say more, forthwith gave the signal, and the executioner did his office.

The popular appeal of executions encouraged a market for eyewitness accounts of notorious cases. Covington's qualified: the news sheet title of 'A true and authentic account of the trial and dying behaviour of Giles Covington' left the potential purchaser in no doubt that this information, hot off the press, was a must-have item! The writer was of a very different opinion from *Jackson's* and the *Gazette* about Covington's 'dying behaviour'. Far from being 'exceedingly agitated', he 'maintained an undaunted resolution to the last', according to the news sheet, and indeed showed behaviour which was 'decent and becoming in every particular excepting his not acknowledging the murder' in Daniel Harris' sympathetic assessment.

The newspapers discounted Covington's protestations of innocence, citing the unsubstantiated fact that he had tried to bribe one of his accusers as further proof of his guilt. Their concluding sentence was a typical appeal to the moral sensibilities of the reader, saying: 'We have only to lament the wickedness and depravity of human nature, that any hardened wretches should thus dare, in their dying moments, by attempting to impose upon credulous minds, insult an already offended deity.'

This unwavering condemnation would have been very much to the authorities' satisfaction, in view of its likely influence on those people still unconvinced of the justice of the verdict. And there were plenty of them, as Harris showed in his post-execution letter to Willoughby, saying there 'could be no secrecy observed ... for I hear tis generally spoken of up town'. Indeed, the papers' moralising sentiments could hardly have been closer to Christopher Willoughby's heart if he had written them himself – which in part is probably what in fact he had done! The papers thought Covington's admission of perjury was sufficient to 'remove every doubt, could any remain, of his guilt'. A few days before, Harris had used those identical words of 'remove every doubt' when suggesting that Willoughby should bring his influence to bear on a susceptible press. Seriously concerned that neither the case against Covington, nor even that against Shury and Castle, had been resolved to the satisfaction of all, Harris had suggested that some pre-emptive action was needed to

> remove every doubt (if any still suppose them innocent) from their minds. But I think some well directed paragraph should appear in the newspapers, to <u>entirely</u> clear up the business. Notwithstanding it may not appear to be absolutely necessary, the circumstance of all three persisting in their innocence at the last moment causes some to have their doubts, I apprehend.

Harris probably felt he was simply doing his duty. There is no sense of vindictiveness in his actions, as his sympathetic references to Covington in the same letter show. In any case the ploy was only partially successful. How furious he must have been to see the hugely significant additional text to which the *Gazette* treated the residents of Berkshire: the very letter that Covington threw down from the scaffold. Its contents did nothing to appease the doubtful:

> What I have now to say cannot be of any further service to me in this world, than by affording me the satisfactory reflection of having done my duty for the few remaining hours I have to stay in it. For that purpose, I have made a full confession of my transgressions and errors, to prevent others from being blamed for what I have committed. There only remains now for me to do justice to myself, by solemnly and truly declaring, in the presence of Almighty God, my entire innocence of the transaction for which I now suffer. My prosecutors

and false accusers I pardon sincerely; but I caution all young and unthinking people from forming any connections, or keeping company with Kilby, or the other two who have falsely sworn away my life, lest, for their own purposes, they should take advantage of an unwary heart, and bring them into the same calamity, which has undeservedly fallen upon me.

This was potent stuff, showing Covington, with his appearance of genuine remorse and concern for others, in the most favourable light yet. Not only that: by printing the letter, the Reading paper was casting very public doubt on the Crown's star witness. The *Gazette's* editor was evidently one of those people still entertaining doubts (albeit managing cleverly to include them in an article which was generally condemnatory). Perhaps there was even an element of partisanship, the paper defending a Berkshire boy accused of an Oxfordshire crime? It is not clear whom Covington meant by the 'other two' false witnesses, but William Bossom, the Oxford bargeman whom Castle had accused of false testimony, seems likely to be one.

The means by which this letter came to be made public is unknown. As too is its authorship. The erudite nature of the composition shows that it was not composed by the semi-literate Covington himself, because the letter that he *did* write, in the two days between his trial and execution, was in a very different style.

Addressed expressly to Christopher Willoughby, it contains much the same sentiments of selfless concern, in the context of a resigned but determined plea of innocence. And it is all the more persuasive for its rudimentary style – although the circumstances under which this letter was penned may give a false impression of Covington's standard of education. Alone in the dark, dank, cold conditions of the Castle, and with the image of the noose in his thoughts, anyone could be forgiven a few grammatical errors and meaningless phrases! The original spelling is phonetic, with words like 'conscience' spelled 'conshonsh' and 'innocent' as 'hinhersent', and what follows is much amended.

Consarn this horred afer with i ham in
oxon Casel for oral Last with is Laid to
My Charge Ther is no douct Ser you
bin at a dal of Trobel a lot it &
a dael of exspenc bot Sr villabe hou
happey tis for me to go to this on timle
fnd vich i exspaks in a short tim
and to Col god to be a witness & hee to
deniit for me vich i Can vich a Safte
Conshonsh i thank god for it
Ther is no dot the poor man Lost is Lifte
Bot Ser villabe it not fond out it
and fou you old find vend tis to Late for
me lot bot it only Ser Taking my Life
Thor is the poor vidder that vill bee Left to
goe and the vide vorld and my Poor mother
and Feather vith Sorow to ther Graves lot the
hoat to make ther Selfs happey mor so
Then if I had bin Giltey of it vith I han
Not I think god

I hope you and your Famley vill Live to
Find that Giles Freeman Covington did
hinhersent and Then I hop you old releve
the vidder that Left lind if beedlum
is not her dom inostid of pitting my
Life bin gon vich will be of no servis
So no mor from
tho unfortnet youth Giles Freeman
I hope god vill bee with   Covington
you and yours

Extract from Covington's moving death-cell letter.
(*Copyright: Oxfordshire Record Office*)

Sir, I have to trouble you with these few lines concerning this horrid affair which I am in Oxon Castle for, or at least which is laid to my charge. There is no doubt, Sir, you been at a deal of trouble about it and a deal of expense, but, Sir Willabe, how happy tis for me to go to this untimely end, which I expect in a short time, and to call God to be a witness, and he to deny it for me, which I can with a safe conscience, I thank God for it.

There is no doubt but the poor man lost his life, but, Sir Willabe, it not found out it, and so you will find when tis too late for me. But it not only, Sir, taking my life. There is the poor widow that will be left to God and the wide world, and my poor mother and father with sorrow to their graves, but the how to make their selfs happy, more so than if I had been guilty of it, which I am not, I thank God.

I hope you and your family will live to find that Giles Freeman Covington died innocent, and then I hope you will relieve the widow that left behind if Bedlam is not her doom, instead of pitying my life, being gone, which shall be of no service. So no more[1] from the unfortunate youth, Giles Freeman Covington. I hope God will be with you and yours.

➤➤ 'Beware of Kilby!' ◄◄

Covington had seemingly been far more riled than the others by Kilby's treachery. He never denied being present when the murder was committed, but was genuinely indignant at the role that Kilby, and only Kilby, allotted him in the drama. Covington's very public resentment of Kilby would soon be widely talked of – and not only locally. The London news sheet writer picked up on this theme too, saying that Covington 'on the platform at the place of execution,

---

1 Here, somewhat poignantly, Covington had written the words 'at present', then crossed them out.

threw down a paper, that he desired might be read aloud, in which he declared himself innocent of the murder, and begged that every person would beware of Kilby'. Daniel Harris had a similar recollection. In the same letter which underlined the need for that 'well-directed paragraph' in the papers, Harris told Willoughby: 'He spoke not a word upon the scaffold, but threw down a paper which expressed that he had left behind a full confession of all his offences, but that he was innocent of what he was going to suffer for, concluding beware of Kilby.'

With Covington dead, only one man knew what really happened that October evening three and a half years earlier: Richard Kilby. Technically he was now a free man, but, given the backgrounds of the many men whom he had betrayed, and the very public doubts about the reliability of his evidence, he could hardly have been popular with either his former comrades or his new masters. Neither Oxford nor Abingdon were places to resume his life, therefore, so he left the district without delay. It was not just a pardon which Kilby was given, but a promise of financial assistance too. Whether this constituted the statutory reward for capital convictions, advertised when the murder was first announced, or whether it smacks of something more underhand, is not clear. Certainly it was not unexpected, as Harris's letter to Willoughby of 27 March 1791 shows:

> Kilby has wrote to me to say that he has got work at Cotton End near Northampton, that he at present lodges in a public house, and wishes me to send him some money that may help him buy goods to go into a private house. I would be guided what answer to send, but I can't help thinking his application somewhat too early.

And there, with possibly the most guilty man of all about to set up a new life in Northamptonshire, the evidence has almost all been presented. No-one will ever know what really happened that October evening, but even from the little that is known of the four protagonists, it is possible to make a reasonable guess.

➤➤ Dying 'with a lie in my mouth' ◄◄

The mature, well-connected Shury was undoubtedly the instigator of both Charteris' murder and much, much more besides. Cunning and persuasive, he seems to have had a hand in almost every bit of skullduggery that Abingdon had to offer at this particular time.

About Kilby, that person of 'ill name and ill fame', there can be little doubt either. Shury tried to strike a deal with him, after all, to pin the blame on the others. And if Shury thought that Kilby was capable of double-crossing two men, he was certainly capable of double-crossing three!

It is less easy to draw conclusions about Castle and Covington. Castle comes across as probably the least guilty, involved only in very petty thefts, taking no physical part in the murder, and racked with conscience over it.

And then there is Covington: a young, impressionable victim of circumstances, courted by the others for his physical prowess? Or a rebellious, aggressive youth, determined to shun his father's law-abiding, conventional footsteps whatever the cost?

The surviving archive evidence provides more clues about Covington than the others. And much of what it says casts him in a favourable light: his naval record, the sympathetic words of Daniel Harris, his evocative letters, his concern for his family … And there was also one final document kept by Christopher Willoughby, a letter from a man with absolutely nothing to gain from entering into the controversy, a Wallingford attorney called **Robert Lovegrove**. As it is undated, we shall never know if this letter was received by Willoughby before or after Covington's death, or whether Willoughby – by all accounts a fair and honourable man – took any action because of it. Whatever, this late contribution to the puzzle attributes to Covington words of a highly intriguing nature:

There is a shopkeeper of respectable character named Joseph Dead-man at Brightwell, Berks, near this place, who was some time since in Oxford Castle, and on observing to Giles Covington (with whom he had been once in company at Sutton) that "he was sorry to see him in that situation" his answer was so remarkable, that out of love to public justice, I thought it necessary to send it to you. "I shall follow the rest of them and die with a lie in my mouth as they did."

What exactly was this 'lie' then, which united all three of them to the last? It was clearly not a reference to their joint claims of inno-cence, so the most likely explanation involves a withholding of evidence, rather than a fabrication. And if that was the case, Peter Pickman's fleeting, half-heard reference to the 'woman who was like-wise present' springs to mind. If a woman really was present – who knows, perhaps one with a particular grudge against Charteris; perhaps even one who struck the fatal blow, with that hedge stake valued at a single penny – it is possible that a sense of chivalry might have united the men in silence. It would be a charitable conclusion to draw about men who, it is possible to believe, were the victims of their own alcohol-fuelled quests for adventure rather than being truly 'moved and seduced by the instigation of the Devil'.

✦ Postscript ✦

After Covington's execution on Monday 7 March 1791, his corpse, like those of Shury and Castle, was used for the furtherance of medical science, the papers stating that:

> After being cut down, the body was delivered, conformably to the Statute of the 25th of the late King,[1] to be anatomised and dissected, and on Tuesday, Dr Pegge, Reader of Anatomy in this University, gave a publick lecture upon the body in the Anatomy School at Christ Church.

How the **Anatomy School** disposed of Castle and Shury's bodies is unknown, but some 150 years later, three skeletons stood outside the office of the Secretary of the Oxford University Museum. One was labelled 'Anglo Saxon', one 'Andaman Islander', and one 'English-man'. The Englishman's skeleton had an identity, the name 'Giles Covington' having been written on the left mandible. By some quirk of fate, Covington's skeleton had been retained intact, albeit with the top of the skull sawn through, and had been displayed at the Museum ever since it opened in the mid-nineteenth century. At some point it was put into store, emerging again as a public exhibit in the early 1980s, this time at the Museum of Oxford.

In 1991, staff at the Museum unsuccessfully sought an official pardon. The evidence used was the same 25 pieces of archive paper-work retained by Christopher Willoughby, and used as the basis of this book. The additional material contained here helps present the context and consequences of the murder of David Charteris more thoroughly than then, and provides greater understanding of the motives and characters of the men involved (or not!). Essentially, though, the fundamental clues to the mystery are all still contained in those few letters, jottings, and incomplete confessions. They were insufficient to prove Covington's innocence in 1791 and 1991, and, despite the additional evidence presented here, are still insufficient today. This book may not have done much to strengthen Covington's case in 2003, therefore, but it has certainly, I hope, also done nothing to diminish it!

1 i.e. the 25th year of George II's reign, meaning 1751.

APPENDIX I:
People named in the text

-+>-<+-

The year of birth has always been assumed as the same as the year of the christening. Where it is followed by a question mark, this indicates a deduction made from the age given at the time of death or some other occasion.

Abbreviations used are:

C	=	Culham	StN	= St Nicholas', Abingdon
D	=	Dorchester	S	= Sutton
MB	=	Marsh Baldon	TB	= Toot Baldon
N	=	Nuneham	WA	= Wallingford
StH	=	St Helen's, Abingdon	W	= Warborough

Basden, William: (?–1817) One of the three bargemen who originally testified against Castle, he was living at 82 Butchers Row when buried in 1817 (StN).

Bossom, William: (1753–1813) The Oxford bargeman whom Castle accused of false testimony just before his execution. The Bossom family was one of the most important in terms of the river trade, especially upstream of Oxford. It was also one of the most prolific, meaning that many individuals named William Bossom were alive at this time. Most probably the man referred to is the William who was one of three brothers to capitalise on the business opportunities presented by the new Oxford Canal in the 1790s, and whose descendants continued to exert a major influence on the Oxford waterway scene for another century and a half. More about the colourful Bossom family appears in the Oxford Towpath Press publication, *A Towpath Walk In Oxford*.

Carter, James: (1748–?) The Nuneham man who was identified as an early prime suspect was probably the James who was christened in 1748 as a son of John and Frances (TB), or who married Mary Shepherd in 1768 when still a 'minor of Toot Baldon' (MB). The implication of this is that Mary was older than James – considerably so if she was the Mary Carter who was buried in 1812, aged 80 (N). They had a son, James, christened in 1769, but he presumably did not survive, since another was christened in 1779 (both N).

Castle, John: (1759?–1790) Castle's age was given as 35 in the description of him issued in 1790, but 31 in the Calendar of Prisoners at Oxford Castle, which is more likely to be accurate. Castle was the only one of the four men accused of the Charteris murder not to have been born in Abingdon. He had been in Abingdon since at least his twenties, however, as he married his first wife, Hannah Mayo (1760–1786) on 12 August 1781 (StH). The Mayos had a recorded presence in Abingdon going back to the mid-sixteenth century, and at least two of Hannah's male relatives – Richard and James – were bargemen, which is no doubt how the match with Castle evolved.

Hannah was buried at St Helen's on 10 March 1786, probably as a result of complications after the birth of their fourth child, John, in February. Assuming some of his young children survived, there was considerable onus on Castle to remarry when Hannah died, which he did on 20 December 1787 (StH). His second wife was Susannah Goodman, whose father, Henry, also worked on the barges.

Like Kilby, Castle may have had a previous conviction, if he was the same John Castle who stole coal from John Collins the younger in 1784. The Collins family was among the principal barge owners of Abingdon, so the connection is more than likely. The coal was valued at ten pence (the equivalent of half a hundredweight or so), and he was sentenced to six weeks in Abingdon Gaol for his aberration.

When arrested at the end of May 1790, Castle admitted to a number of other thefts. He was probably hoping for leniency, but was also carrying out his threat – in the phrase attributed to him almost

word for word by the other bargemen – to bring down those who
'held their heads high' in Abingdon. Yet this incriminating list is only
in the form of rough notes, not a confession as such. Indeed, no first-
person statement by either Castle or Shury survives, so it is difficult to
know if Castle remained loyal to Covington and Kilby, whose names
are conspicuously missing from the list, or if it is simply the confession
itself which is missing. What *is* clear is that he had no intention of
sparing Shury's blushes.

In all, Castle spilled out the names of at least 12 men, involved
either in pilferage or procurement of goods from boats, the theft of
wine from The George public house in Shillingford, a pig taken from
Marcham Mills, or the preferred booty of pigeons and poultry.
Shury's name was prominent, as too was that of a bargeman called
William Jarrett. Other Abingdon men likely to have kept their heads
very much *down* in the months to come were a weaver called Thomas
Pearce, a bargeman called Richard May, and James Battin, Mr
Mathew Phillips, Isaac Evans, Isaac Evans the younger, William
Pratt, Joseph Crawford, and John Crawford. Castle also named some
victims: the publican Mr Powell, Mr Elwes of Marcham, Mr James
Bridgeman of Sutton, Mr (Lawrence?) Wyatt of Drayton, Mr Ashby
of Shillingford, and Mrs Browne of Wittenham.

Charteris, David: (?–1787) Other than at his burial at Toot Baldon
on 13 October 1787, David Charteris (also spelled Charters, Chartres,
and Charteres) appears in no other of the parish records searched.
He does appear once in the Oxfordshire Quarter Sessions records,
however, when (spelled Charters) he parted with £27 2s on 27 November 1780 on behalf of one Henry Townsend. So the two abiding
historical references to Charteris, a supposed poor travelling linen
draper, involve large sums of money! Trade cannot have been too
bad, as shown by the auction of his goods in January 1788. The notice
in *Jackson's* specified 'Irish linens of various widths and prices, ⅞ and
¾ Dowlas; printed cottons and linens; men's, women's, and youths'
worsted, cotton and thread hose, with a variety of goods in the

mercery, drapery and haberdashery business. Also beds, bedsteads, tables, chairs, and a variety of household furniture.'

Trading in linen was an obvious choice for a resident of Toot Baldon. In his survey of Oxfordshire agriculture, Arthur Young noted in 1807 that 'it is not 40 years ago since every cottage at Baldon had a plot of hemp, and all manufactured into linen for their own consumption, selling what they could spare: at present, no such thing; the last was given up about six years ago.' He noted other recent changes in the agricultural practices of Christopher Willoughby's tenants too, saying that: 'Formerly, many cottagers about Baldon had two, three, or four acres, and they kept cows' but they had then turned over the land to arable. This change was symptomatic of a major dietary change which affects us still: 'A few years ago, they had no potatoes; now all have them. Formerly they did not like that root with their bacon, only cabbage: at present they are generally eaten.'

At some point in the murder investigation, the following information was jotted down: 'People fixed on by Shury to be robbed going from Abingdon market: Wise of Abingdon, Curtis of Northcot, Stevens of Steventon'. Under other circumstances, evidently, Charteris might have been spared his fate that evening, and lived to learn of another man's misfortune a few days later with no inkling of his own narrow escape!

Covington, Giles Freeman: (1767–1791) Unlike his three older brothers, Giles never exhibited the skills, patience, or application to merit an apprenticeship. His was a much more wayward nature, so that (as the news sheet covering his execution put it):

> The connecting himself with loose company very early led him to have an aversion to confinement, hence he had a dislike to the business of a taylor, in which he was instructed by his father, and at length was associated with the unmerciful and profligate wretches who committed this horrible murder, when he was but 18 years of age.

How true this was is debatable. There is no way of knowing just how impressionable Covington was, nor how much influence the older men had on him. He was indeed only 18 when he and Shury committed arguably the most audacious of all the crimes uncovered in this history, the theft of the silverware from St Nicolas' Church in 1785. This was followed by the unsubstantiated accusation of stealing turkeys from one John Hayward in January 1786. A later newspaper report claimed that he worked as a butcher in Oxford at some point. Certainly, this is work which might well have suited him, but it seems more likely that the writer was confusing his occupation with Butcherow, the street in Abingdon (more commonly called Bridge Street, and sometimes Burford Street) in which the parental home lay. Whatever, there is no evidence of Covington ever having gone to Oxford for any occasion other than his own demise.

Two months after the murder, on 18 December 1787, Covington's daughter, Elizabeth, was christened out of wedlock (StH). Given his father's prominent place in Abingdon affairs, one can imagine Roger Covington's dismay on learning that this, his third grandchild, was illegitimate. The public humiliation must have been considerable, not least for the 19-year-old mother, Ann Gilkes. Nonetheless, the idea of marriage seems to have been resisted by someone, because Elizabeth had seen her first birthday before Giles and Ann tied the knot. Breaking with both families' traditions, the wedding was at St Nicholas' on 5 February 1789 (the banns having been read on 28 September, 5 October and 12 October 1788). This and the absence of any Covingtons among the witnesses suggests a family rift, and possible disownment by Roger Covington of his youngest son.

When Covington left Abingdon at some point between November 1789 and May 1790, London was a natural choice. Here, notwithstanding the increasing effectiveness of the officers of Bow Street, a wanted man could melt with ease into anonymity amidst the confusing sprawl of the capital's suburbs. For Covington the choice was even more obvious, as London was the home of numerous relatives. Most were in Aldersgate, Holborn, and Queenhithe, and Ann Covington gave her address as St Botolph, Aldersgate when their son, Gyles, was christened at St Sepulchre's, Holborn on 11 June 1790. It was no coincidence that this was the very church where a certain Roger Covington been christened in 1729.

Covington, Roger: (1729–1798) Giles Covington's father seems to have moved to Abingdon in his twenties. There is no record of his marriage in Abingdon, which suggests he moved to Abingdon with his wife, Elizabeth, soon before the birth of their first child in 1755. What attracted him to Abingdon is anyone's guess – although the river, an influence running steadily through this history, provides one logical rationale. Only a matter of half a mile from St Sepulchre's and the Covingtons' adjacent heartland of Aldersgate was Bull Wharf, Queenhithe. In 1773 (according to a notice in *Jackson's*), and presumably earlier, this wharf near Southwark Bridge was the only one in London where barges from Oxford loaded. The crews would therefore all be familiar with Abingdon, which lay on or close to their route. Additionally, some of the Covington family actually lived in Queenhithe from at least 1759. This included Richard Covington (a second cousin of Giles, the two sharing the same great-grandfather), who became a Thames lighterman (authorised to manoeuvre lighters – small, flat-bottomed boats – through the crowded waters of the tidal Thames) in 1780.[1] So perhaps Roger came to learn of Abingdon through the opportunity to talk to the Oxford bargemen, and learn of the attractions of life in a small riverside town. Or perhaps he was already a tailor, his occupation in Abingdon from at least 1768, and had dealings with the Abingdon merchants whose cloth was bound for the expanding clothing industry of London's East End. It is quite possible, as his father William (1703–?), though a farrier by trade, had been apprenticed to the Haberdashers Company as a boy.

---

1 Richard (and at least one other of the family) went on to build a successful career in this highly skilled profession. In contrast to an uncle of Roger's called Peter (1706–?), who was transported from Newgate to Maryland in 1725. Giles was obviously not the only black sheep in the family!

So what drew Roger to Abingdon is not certain, but the river may well have played its part. It seems likely too that the very aspect of London life which Giles saw as his salvation was what Roger wanted to evade. He was by all accounts an honourable and honest man, and these were not necessarily attributes compatible with the cut-throat world of eighteenth-century east London. The comparable attractions of Abingdon for a young man about to start a family must have been considerable. Whatever his incentive, if Roger Covington hoped that by moving to he Abingdon would ensure an honest upbringing for his family, he was only partially right. His first three sons did well for themselves. His youngest son, Giles, of course, did not.

Edward (1755–1805) became a successful baker. John (1757–?) was apprenticed to his father in 1772, but was an alehousekeeper from at least October 1787 and ran a prestigious Abingdon inn, The Chaise and Horses, by the end of the century. Thomas (1762–1838?) pursued his father's trade, and to great effect. By the end of the century, though living in London, he owned six tenements in Abingdon as well as premises in Boar Street in 1803 and in Bury Lane in 1810. At the time of his death, supposed at 1838 from the date of his will, his address was a London one, even though he was described as a 'gentleman of Abingdon'. Thomas did most to ensure the Covington line by having six children between 1786 and 1805.

Giles Freeman, Roger's youngest son, was christened on 12 April 1767 (StH). The next year Roger was eligible to vote, and although this suggests he acquired his freedom at this time, and celebrated the fact with Giles' middle name, no record of such appears in the Borough Minutes. The family seem to have lived in Butcherow (also known as Bridge Street and Burford Street) from then on. In 1783 the property was described as 'a messuage or tenement and shop with appurtenances in the Butcherow on the east side', and Roger appears to have remained there till his death.

On 21 June 1780 Roger was elected to the prestigious post of Bellman. The role was a responsible and varied one, for which he received from the Borough a salary of £8, with an additional £1 10s 'for turning vagrants out of town' and £5 for himself 'and one able bodied man to assist him in the nightly watch'. This important civic role comprised many other duties too, mostly remunerated on a case by case basis. These were listed in full when Richard Gilkes (Ann Gilkes' brother) assumed the post after Roger's death in September 1798, and included a requirement to attend the Mayor at church and other public events; to clean and light the public lamps; to clean the Corporation's cutlery; to maintain its fire engine; to clean and care for the Market House and its surrounds, and 'to see that the scavenger do take the filth away'. On being elected, Roger signed a declaration agreeing 'not to keep a common alehouse or sell ale, beer or any other strong liquor', and was issued with a special coat, hat, and badge. Conveniently, he made the coat himself! The nature of this uniform is clarified in the Borough minutes of June 1783: 'a new laced hat, a new cloke, and new coat, waistcoat, breeches and stockings of blue colour as formerly'.

The Bellman's duties also included procuring various quantities (called 'assizes') of bread every year for distribution (generally by his son, Edward) to the poor of the Borough. He was also paid for arranging bonfires on occasions of particular importance. In March 1789 it was a bonfire with a difference. George III was a popular monarch, but subject to sudden and unpredictable bouts of mental illness. So *Jackson's* was pleased to record on 14 March 1789 'the happy restoration of his Majesty's health ... and resumption of his royal authority'. It was the cue for celebrations on a national scale, and in Abingdon the event was marked 'by the ringing of bells, bonfires and a general illumination, with many curious emblematical devices and every demonstration of zealous attachment'. Beer was distributed to the populace, and copies of a national newspaper containing a 'false and execrable libel on Majesty ... was consigned to be burnt publicly by the Common Cryer in the Market Place'. This 'Common' (or Town) Cryer was Roger Covington, one of his most frequent duties of all being to announce to a largely illiterate populace any new laws, borough regulations, or other items of essential public interest. Even with these seemingly endless calls on Covington's time, day and night, he still managed to keep his needle busy, and was paid 10s in 1785 to replace his own uniform. He therefore obviously truly was the 'industrious honest man' the *Gazette* described him as in 1791 – although even he was not without a streak of mischief. Yet another of the Bellman's roles was to attend the law courts. As 'Hall-keeper of the County Court' he was forced to make a public apology in *Jackson's* of 19 October 1782 to twelve members of a jury whom he had locked up 'for the space of two hours after they had agreed on their verdict, and also did ridicule and laugh at said jury under their confinement'.

Crawford, Betsy/Elizabeth (née Gleed): (1732? or 1740? – ?) The landlady of The Magpye in 1790 and 1796 was probably the Elizabeth Gleed 'of Culham' who married William Crawford (of Oxford) in 1759, and had children baptised in 1771 and 1773, and possibly also in 1761 (all StN). She seems certain too to have been the Elizabeth baptised in either 1732 (C) or 1740 (C) to Bennett and Mary Gleed, the father being described as a 'bargeman' from 1738 (StH) onwards. A relative, George Gleed, described as 'of Culham' when buried in 1807 (StN), was one of only 250 Berkshire residents eligible to vote in county elections in 1768. In 1795, he owned a barge called the *Abingdon* with the enormous capacity of 130 tons, and in 1796 was one of four Abingdon barge owners operating to Brooks Wharf (today's Broken Wharf?) at Queenhithe in London. The others were Betsy Crawford herself, Peter Pickman, and Edward Child (like Pickman, also a brewer).

Crawford, Joseph: (1749–1835) Joe was a cousin or brother of Betsy's husband William, both men hailing from the waterside parish of St Thomas in Oxford, where Joe was christened in 1749. By 1771, when he married Mary Glanvil (StN), he was described as being 'of Culham'. He became a bargemaster in his own right at some point, but nothing more is evident about this couple until their deaths, when Joseph was buried aged 87 in 1835 and Mary aged 89 in 1837 (both StN, and both then residing at 'Abbey').

Field, Mrs: probably Anne 'of Burcot', who with her husband Richard had many children between 1739 and 1763 (D).

Gilkes, Ann: (1768–1791) Giles Covington's future wife was christened on 14 April 1768 (StH), the fourth of a family of eight born between 1761 and 1779. Like Roger Covington, Ann's father Thomas (1729?–1787) seems to have been the first of his family to live in Abingdon. He achieved his freedom in 1759, and the christening of Thomas' oldest son Richard (1761–1813) is the earliest appearance of the name in St Helen's parish records. Thomas was a plumber and glazier, a notoriously hazardous profession on account of the fatal effects of frequent exposure to lead, and both Thomas and his brother, another plumber and glazier of Watlington, went to relatively early graves, as too did Thomas' wife, Ann (?–1786).

With both her parents dead before her 19th birthday, it was her brother Richard who gave Ann away at her wedding to Giles Covington at St Nicholas' on 5 February 1789. She had acquired enough education to sign her name on the wedding certificate, but seems not to have been quite sane. Why else would Covington, in his death-cell letter to Christopher Willoughby, express the fear that she might be consigned to Bedlam rather than a poor house? The pernicious effects of lead poisoning are apparent again perhaps, and Ann's tragic life was soon over anyway. The couple's illegitimate daughter Elizabeth died of smallpox in August 1790 (StH), while Giles was at sea, and their son Gyles seems certain also to have died in infancy. Ann herself was buried on 27 September 1791 (StH), only a few months after her husband's demise.

If life as a plumber and glazier was a hazardous one, it was also lucrative. Thomas' eldest son Richard took over the business when his father died, and was living in a house of considerable size in Lombard Street by 1797. Wisely, Richard changed his profession in his thirties, however, and there is a certain poignancy in the role he subsequently adopted as Abingdon's Bellman on the death of Roger Covington in September 1798.

Goodman, Susannah: (1769– ?) Castle married Susannah Goodman on 20 December 1787 (StH), a few months after Charteris' murder. Every eighteenth-century Abingdon family seems to have had its black sheep. In the case of the Shurys, it was Charles Evans; for the Covingtons, Giles Freeman; and for the Goodmans, it seems to have been Susannah's father, Henry (1739–1818). Henry's name appeared in the papers three times, and on no occasion was it any cause for pride. When two men ironically described in *Jackson's* of 30 November 1765 as 'two of those gentry who call themselves *Horse Takers*' were arrested, Goodman was named as the third member of the gang. He was also attributed the alias 'Cherry', the similarity to 'Jerre', the name used by the illiterate Kilby, being convincingly close. It was presumably the same Henry Goodman who was committed to Oxford Castle two years later on a charge, later dropped, of stealing a ewe from Crowmarsh. Now a married man, he was in trouble again in 1777, being one of the 19 men obliged to make a public apology to Lord Harcourt in *Jackson's* of 8 March 1777. After hauling a barge upstream to Nuneham Lock, which lay immediately below Nuneham House, they had broken down some railings and trespassed on Harcourt's land on the way back. The official towing path lay on the opposite bank, but the men had decided to return along the eastern side of the river. The reason may well have been one which is rarely far away in this history – alcohol! T. Hewitt, the Waterturnpike House publican, presumably, was one of the 19 and the idea of stopping at his establishment after their hard work would no doubt have appealed! Goodman classed himself as a bargemen (at least in 1786), so this is no doubt how he and John Castle became acquainted. He is one of many examples of Abingdon men whose right to vote was not necessarily an indication of conformity, honesty, or wealth.

Susannah was christened on 21 March 1769 (StH), the eldest of nine children born between 1769 and 1786 – although at least six of her siblings appear to have died in infancy, indicative of the poverty which classed her father among the 'parish poor' at this time. Susannah was only 18 when she married, and seems likely to have had to care for the children from Castle's first marriage, as well as a couple of younger brothers and sisters. It could not have been easy, with a husband who was often (and then permanently, from March 1790) away on the river.

If there ever really was 'a woman who was likewise present' when Charteris was killed, Susannah would be the prime candidate. Castle, drunk as he probably was when he first confided in his fellow bargemen, would not have wanted to mention his own wife by name. And with her youth, family ties, impoverishment, and young dependants, it is not inconceivable that all the men might have felt inclined to protect her identity, had she been there, and to die with what Covington called that 'lie in my mouth'.

Harcourt, George Simon: (1736–1809) The Harcourt family had owned Nuneham House and Park since 1710, and had altered it considerably by the end of the century, under the influence of Simon, the 1st Earl (1714–1777), and his son, George Simon (1736–1809). Having decided to make Nuneham (spelled Newnham until 1749) his main residence, the 1st Earl was responsible for a major transformation of the estate, which involved construction of the current village in the 1760s and building a perimeter wall over six miles in length. Soon after the death of Simon, described in *Jackson's* as 'a nobleman of an amiable and irreproachable character, of the most engaging politeness, and exemplary in all the duties of private life', the appearance of the estate was further enhanced by Capability Brown. Like his father, George Simon held high public office, and both he and his wife Elizabeth became favourites of King George III and Queen Charlotte, rising to the positions of Master of the King's Horse and Lady of the Bedchamber respectively. This accounts for the many royal visits made to Nuneham in the 1780s, and would have made the authorities all the more keen to solve a murder which had occurred altogether rather 'too close to home' for comfort.

Harris, Daniel: (1760?–1840) As Governor of the County Gaol at Oxford Castle from 1786 to 1809, Harris presided at a time of national prison reform and a period when the dilapidated prison walls were undergoing much-needed rebuilding. He was the perfect man for the job: promoted from Clerk of Works in his mid-twenties, he had previously trained as a carpenter, and exhibited both engineering and building skills which were doubtless useful in making the Castle site secure. It was these skills which brought him to the attention of the waterways authorities, both on the River Thames and the new Oxford Canal, which opened in 1790. And it was not only engineering flair that Harris had to offer, but also cheap and plentiful labour in the form of the convicts under his care.

Abingdon had a vested interest in Harris' efforts. When the Oxford Canal opened on New Year's Day 1790, Oxford found itself on the shortest water route between the newly industrialising Midlands and London. Abingdon lay on that same route, and the bargemen and merchants of the town would soon feel the benefit. Harris must have been something of a puzzle to them: an authority figure familiar with Oxford's commercial and political elite, yet from an artisan background which might also have facilitated a rapport with the working boatmen. Certainly there was probably no-one better placed to round up those members of the close-knit boating community 'in the know', when rumours of Castle's involvement in the murder surfaced in April 1790. Daniel Harris remained a regular choice for waterway projects in the Oxford area for over a decade, and became thereby a pivotal figure in the social and economic development of Oxford at a time of particular change and innovation. More about Harris – who could count being an illustrator, builder, architect, and (on the Castle site where he resided) even an amateur archaeologist amongst his other attributes – appears in *A Towpath Walk In Oxford* published by Oxford Towpath Press.

Hewitt, Thomas: (1736?–1824) At this time of widespread illiteracy, surnames were often recorded with slight variations of spelling. Hewitt, the man responsible for the Waterturnpike House in October 1787, acquired more versions than most, appearing variously as Heart,

Hewet, Hewett, and Hearett. The most likely candidate is Thomas Hewitt, who married Sarah Bowles in 1760 (C). Thomas and Sarah had numerous children from 1763 onwards. Thomas was 88 when he died in 1824 (StH), having survived his wife by exactly 20 years.

Jackson, Thomas: (1744?–1819) The man who found Charteris' body and attended the trial was also one of the twelve men, probably all from either Nuneham Courtenay or Toot Baldon, summoned to witness the Coroner William Johnson's inquest. He and his wife Elisabeth were granted legal settlement in Toot Baldon in 1774, and had children christened in 1775 and 1784 (MB). He was buried aged 75 in 1819 (TB).

Johnson, William: (?–1791) One of the Coroners for Oxfordshire from 1752 to 1791, Johnson lived in Benson, about six miles along the road to Reading, when called upon to examine Charteris' corpse in Nuneham. Although Johnson's role in this history is a small, official one only, it is worth recounting one or two of his more unusual cases to give a flavour of the varied and responsible role of an eighteenth-century coroner at a time of rudimentary forensic knowledge.

The earliest reference to him came in *Jackson's* of 30 March 1754. It was as gruesome a case as he was ever likely to encounter, an inquest into the death of a young child found near Nettlebed 'with its throat cut from ear to ear, and the left arm and the right leg cut off close to the body'.

In July 1768 he attended the drowned body of Thomas Crumplin, 'a boy belonging to a barge', at Henley and was called to Oxford Castle in October 1773 on account of a young prisoner who had gone to bed at ten o'clock the previous night in perfect health, but became suddenly ill and expired before midnight.

One of Johnson's most disturbing cases came in 1785, when he delivered a verdict of 'accidentally drowned' on John Prince, the Abingdon Bridewell Keeper, who had been missing for nearly two months. Johnson felt it necessary to call in a surgeon first, though, because it was known that Prince's life had been threatened 'by some evil-disposed persons who had been his prisoners', and a swelling on his head showed possible signs of violence. At the time, nothing was proven – as indeed it would have been very difficult to do on a corpse subjected to the winter-time ravages of the Thames for several weeks – but nearly six years later Johnson had the case reopened. Given the difficulties of dealing with even current crimes, this seems an extraordinary step, notwithstanding the official status of the victim. It was justified though, and *Jackson's* of 26 February 1791 announced that 'one – Evans of Abingdon' had been arrested on suspicion of his murder. Subsequently, another name hovering in the wings of this history, William Pratt, was also accused of the murder. Johnson had been fooled originally because the body had 'been buried in sand by the murderers for six weeks, and afterwards by them thrown in the river, that it might be supposed he had accidentally drowned'.

The death of William Bayliss of Ducklington was another unusual case. As rumours of foul play persisted after the funeral, Johnson insisted on having the coffin opened. According to *Jackson's* of 2 February 1788, Bayliss had been drinking with friends in Witney the day before, and had become very violent on the walk home, being 'greatly intoxicated with liquor, to which was addicted, and extremely quarrelsome when so circumstanced'. On questioning, his companions did admit to striking Bayliss, but only with the intention of calming him down. Johnson accepted their plea, but the case caused sufficient consternation for *Jackson's* to caution 'parishes as well as individuals not to suffer persons dying under doubtful circumstances to be buried until an enquiry has been made by the proper officer'.

Kilby, Richard: (1764?–?) Of the four members of Shury's gang, the background of Richard Kilby is the most difficult to pin down with any certainty. In Kilby's case, this is mainly because there were several Richard Kil(l)by's living in the Abingdon area at this time, and to add further confusion, two of them married women called Sarah.

Another difficulty is that Kilby's marital status is never specified in any of the archive documents available. Lastly, the one reference to his age (as 26 in the Calendar of Prisoners issued in July 1790) does not correspond with any of the baptism dates at St Helen's Church, where every Kilby worshipped.

Assessing all the available facts (and assuming that he married at all), Kilby could have been the man who married Sara(h) Bradley on 8 January 1789 (stH). This couple had at least nine children between 1792 and 1811, dates which might fit with a man returning to conventional domesticity in Abingdon after a judicious period of exile in Northamptonshire. It *is* just possible – especially if the town was actually ultimately grateful to Kilby, whatever his other shortcomings, for his part in extinguishing Shury's malign influence. This Kilby served in the Militia in 1798; how likely that would be, in view of Kilby's past desertion, is debatable.

Another Richard Kilby (almost certainly a relative) was a publican from at least 1782, and ran an inn called The Coach and Horses which was prestigious enough to be included in the Universal British Directory of 1796.

So, the parish records reveal frustratingly little about the Richard Kilby who, whatever the truth of the actual case, felt able to look former friends in the eye, and forfeit their lives in exchange for his own. We know from his pardon and Abingdon's Quarter Session records that he was sentenced in May 1785 to spend three months at Abingdon's House of Correction for a theft committed on 4 November 1784. It was this that prompted the important observation that 'Kilby was before convicted', written on the back of Daniel Harris' letter to Willoughby of 22 June 1790. Kilby and others had stolen from William Walker of Kingston Bagpuize ten turkeys, thirteen fowls, five ducks, two geese, two cheesecloths, and a linen bag, valued in total at £11. It was a sizeable haul, and one which could have attracted a much stiffer penalty. Maybe Kilby even then had friends in high places ...

Unsurprisingly it was in an Abingdon alehouse, The Bull, where

Kilby and three others (including a William Kilby, possibly his brother) had met to plan the burglary. For allowing these 'persons of ill name and ill fame' (as they were described in the Quarter Sessions minutes) to gather on her premises, the landlady Mary Stevens too was summoned, with dire consequences for her continued licencee-ship, no doubt. But Kilby's involvement was scarcely a secret anyway. Sixteen men testified to his guilt!

Whoever he was, Kilby, as King's evidence, seems likely to have been detained in Oxford even after the issue of his pardon in September 1790. He was certainly instantly available the day Covington was brought to Oxford, and it is unlikely the authorities would risk letting such an important witness out of their clutches. To judge by one of the prison reformer John Howard's observations, Kilby might well have been lodged at some secure location all this time. Howard noted that in 1782 a felon who had turned King's evidence was being held at the Oxford City Bridewell.

Whether or not he returned to Abingdon while alive, it seems likely that with numerous relatives in the district, Kilby would at least have been laid to rest in his home town once dead. But if the St Helen's marriages and births associated with the Richard Kilby name offer more confusion than clarity, so it is too with the burials. If Kilby returned at all, his burial could be either that of 27 February 1799, or even, allowing for inaccuracies, the man who was buried 'aged 65' in 1823 (both stH).

Latimer, Robert: A resident of Warborough, the only record refers to the funeral of William, the son of Robert and Anne in 1769 (w).

Lovegrove, Robert: Identified only by the letter 'R' in his letter to Christopher Willoughby, the only Wallingford gentleman who fits the bill at this time is Robert, who had five children with his wife Sarah between 1783 and 1791 (wA). He was presumably the same Robert Lovegrove who was listed as an attorney in the Universal British Directory of 1796.

Parker, John?: (1746?–1802) The Christian name and home town of the man who shared a drink with Charteris at the Waterturnpike House on the fateful evening are never specified. It seems likely he came from Dorchester, though, because when they parted company his route took him home over Culham Common and via Burcot. A John Parker married in Dorchester in 1774, and had six children between 1775 and 1802, in which year he was buried, aged 56 (D). His widow, Eleanor, was buried in 1806, aged 49 (D).

Pauper Woman: When the Abingdon boatmen and their associates revealed their versions of what Castle had confessed to in April 1790, they all made reference to a second murder, that of a woman supposedly thrown off Culham Bridge by Castle with assistance from either Kilby or Covington. The incident is never referred to again in any of the evidence, even though Susannah Spicer, a tradesman's wife with an ear for such detail, even remembered the exact value of what was stolen, saying 'there was £10 worth of lace belonging to the woman'. No date is ever attributed to this incident but the burial at Culham of 'a woman casual pauper who was drowned' on 4 April 1788 seems certain to be her.

Peck, Simon: The man whose determination to retrieve his stolen horse proved the undoing of Shury and his gang when his 'laudable spirit, almost regardless of either fatigue or expense', as the *Gazette* put it, resulted in the capture of Thomas 'Oxford Tom' Smith. The Pecks had a long association with Abingdon. It was also a controversial one. From the middle of the seventeenth century, non-conformist gatherings were held at the home of Simon (?–1671) and Katherine (?–1709) Peck, and Katherine continued to host these dangerous meetings after her husband's death despite being excommunicated and imprisoned in London in 1686. The Pecks' malting business gave them sufficient financial security to remain publicly true to their beliefs, however, in alliance with the still wealthier and more influential family of the Tomkins, whose philanthropic legacy for Abingdon has been well documented by other writers.

The absence of Baptist Church records makes it difficult to trace the lineage of the Simon Peck who resided at Rye (or Rivy) Farm. Was he the same man who was paid a salary of £16 'for carrying away the dirt out of the streets' from 1775 till 1788? If so, the position, called 'Scavenger' in the Abingdon Borough Minutes, was seemingly not the demeaning occupation the title might suggest, because Rye Farm was a very substantial property, and Peck a man of rank. He presumably occupied the farm from 1784, following the death that year of the previous owner, Mrs Pope. With occupancy came a responsibility to maintain a footbridge over Swift Ditch, and in 1797 the Borough threatened him with an indictment following his failure to conform with a previous order to repair it in 1795.

Pickman, **Peter**: The Half Moon, where the brewer Peter Pickman overheard the damning rumours of Castle's guilt, was probably his 'local', because his business interests, by 1795/6 anyway, lay firmly in this part of town. He traded then from a prime site near St Helen's Church, by the slipway where East St Helen's Street meets the river. It comprised a wharf, dwelling house, malthouse, and warehouse, and was of sufficient importance to enable Pickman to be included in the Universal British Directory of 1796 as both a brewer and bargemaster. There was probably also an alehouse on the site, as both Benjamin Woolsgrove and another unnamed person mentioned The Wharf House as one of the places they had visited during the critical hours of October 8th 1787. It was this wharf too where many of the petty thefts enumerated by Castle would probably have occurred. Pickman leased the premises from one of Abingdon's most famous and successful families, the Tomkins. One can assume both from this and the general absence of the surname from the local church records that Pickman, like the Tomkins and Peck families, was a Baptist – at least at this time. Several members of the family were buried in St Helen's the following century, including Pickman's wife,

Rebecca (1752?–1818), son, Peter (1767[1]–1843), and daughter-in-law, Fanny (1781–1852), she and Peter having married in 1819 (StN). Of Peter Pickman senior, however, no dates at all are evident.

Pickman was still in occupation of the site in 1799, according to William Tomkins' will of that year, and was trading under the corporate name of William Pickman & Co in 1795, according to Leonard Naylor's 1965 pamphlet on the Tomkins family. It was a common pattern in towns by the Thames to find malting, brewing, and barge ownership combined, and Peter Pickman was one of the four Abingdon barge owners listed in the Universal British Directory of 1796.

Pratt, William: In his statement of 5 April 1790, the bargeman John Brown said that Castle had mentioned stealing from the murdered pauper woman a silver-tipped item, which had been taken to 'the house of William Sprat, a weaver in Littlebury Lane in Abingdon'. William Basden, another of the bargemen interviewed on the same day, mentioned Spra(t)t too, saying that Castle had said 'that they were all drinking in Wm Sprat's house when the gang confessed what they had all done and that Wm Spratt was the person that was the occasion of Mr Peck's mare being stole'. A William Pratt was mentioned in Kilby's confession, and also, as Platt, by Castle – although not in connection with either of the above incidents. As the names Sprat(t) and Platt do not occur in any parish record, it seems likely that all the above refer to the name which does appear: William Pratt. One such individual had a son christened in 1781, and one was buried, a 'labourer', in 1801 (both StN). A William Pratt was also accused with one of the Evans family of murdering John Prince, the Abingdon Bridewell Keeper, in 1785 (see Johnson). It is presumably the same man, or a relative, who was described in *Jackson's* in 1779 as 'about twenty-six years of age, about five feet seven inches high, has light-grey eyes, is well made, remarkably stout and fixed in the knees and legs, and generally goes well and cleanly dressed … His business is

---

1 Suggesting that Rebecca was either Peter Pickman senior's second wife, or a very young mother indeed!

that of a sack-weaver.' Men normally had their descriptions in print for only one reason in the eighteenth century, and Pratt, sure enough, was wanted for a burglary which had occurred in Abingdon three or four years previously. An ostensibly more respectable resident, the currier Lawrence Spicer, had already been arrested on suspicion of the same crime.

Shury, Charles Evans: (1747–1790) The Shury (Shurey/Shewery/Shurt) family had been present in Abingdon since at least the seventeenth century, the earliest reference being found in 1665. The name Charles was traditional in the family from these earliest times. One, probably the grandfather of Charles Evans, died in 1729 (StH). Appropriately enough in a story inseparable from the Thames, this Charles was a 'boatman', or at least had been when he married Ann Weston in 1701 (StH). That river connection would be both profitable for Charles Evans nearly a century later, and, indirectly, fatal.

Charles Evans Shury was baptised on 9 August 1747 (StH), the third child of Jonathan/John (?–1771) 'of St Nicholas' and Elizabeth Badcock (?–1785), who married in 1742 (StH). The Badcocks were also well established in Abingdon, Henry Badcock of 'Norcutt' (Northcourt) being one of a handful of Abingdon freeholders eligible to vote in an election for 'Knights of the Shire' in 1727. The couple had ten other children between 1744 and 1758. Almost all were christened at St Nicholas'. Among the sons was another with the middle name of Evans (William, christened in 1756, reinforcing the notion of a family tie with the men of that surname who feature in this text). On these many brothers and sisters the historical record is silent, and only John (1745–1804) has any bearing on this history. It is a strong one, however, as the fates of the two brothers were intimately entwined.

In their early twenties both Charles and John married within a year of each other. It began a momentous period in the brothers' lives. First Charles married Martha White (?–1773) on 25 October 1769 at St Helen's, then John married an Oxford girl, Elizabeth

White (1748–1772),[1] on 21 June 1770 at St Nicholas'. Eight months later, in February 1771, John Shury senior died (stN). A brewer by trade, it is clear from the rating lists of Abingdon property owners that he was a very successful one. As the oldest son, John was presumably the prime inheritor. Soon after, still in his early thirties, he would inherit again as a result of his marriage. For his wife was an only child and her father, Francis, the proprietor of one of Oxford's most famous inns: The Greyhound (now demolished) at the corner of the High Street and Longwall Street. This was a very substantial building of four storeys, with a history going back to the sixteenth century, and the young couple probably lived there after the marriage, because their daughters were both christened at nearby St Peter's East. Mary was baptised in August 1771 and Ann in August 1772. Tragedy struck with the birth of this second girl, however, as neither mother nor daughter survived for more than a few weeks.

Like John, Charles Evans Shury also lost his wife at an early age. Martha died in April 1773 (stN), leaving him with two young daughters, Ann (who was christened in April 1770) and Martha (in May 1772). For the two Shury brothers, the early 1770s had therefore been punctuated with a succession of church ceremonies of contrasting emotion. By mid-1773, while still in their twenties, their father was dead, they were both widowers, and they both had motherless daughters to care for. There the similarities end. John amassed a fortune, Charles ultimately amassed nothing but misfortune.

As a young man, however, Charles showed none of the criminal tendencies apparent in his later years. He too seems to have benefitted when his father died in February 1771, since it is he and not John (who was living in Oxford then anyway) who is named on the roll of property owners liable to Poor Tax in September 1771. This probably refers to the family home in Stert Street. The same year Charles

---

1 That the two brothers married girls with the same surname is intriguing, especially given Elizabeth's pedigree as a publican's daughter, but no blood tie between the two is apparent.

assumed responsibility for 'looking after the Stert floodgates ... near his house' at the end of Broad Street. It was a trusted position, since the Stert Stream represented a seasonal flooding hazard to some of Abingdon's grandest houses. He fulfilled this civic role for nine years, at a token annual payment of 3s 6d, but in 1780 the Borough decided he should 'be paid nothing for the same in future'. There is no sense of dismissal in this comment; it was merely that keys had been distributed to all the nearby residents, to enable them to take collective responsibility.

Meanwhile, John Shury was moving up in the world. Already the owner of four properties in Abingdon in 1776, three of them valued considerably above the average, his fortune was greatly increased when his father-in-law Francis White died in February 1777, and The Greyhound was sold. John was named in White's will as the joint beneficiary of the residue of his estate plus all his 'stock in business, bills, bonds, book debts, ready money, securities for money ... goods, chattels, and credits'. An advertisement in *Jackson's* of 28 June 1777 shows how substantial The Greyhound – and therefore John's inheritance – was: included in White's effects were 'near forty bedsteads'.

In the October after White's death, John secured his second advantageous connection by marrying Mary Townsend, the eldest daughter of Mr John Townsend, an eminent builder of Oxford. By the time their first child was christened March 1778, John and Mary had moved to Abingdon, and could count themselves among the town's wealthiest residents. Their home was a substantial property in Stert Street, described in 1778 as

> all that messuage or tenement garden ground and backside thereunto belonging, containing at both ends 18 feet extending from the Stert to the Convent Orchard Wall and all Houses and buildings thereunto belonging, situate in the Stert late in the occupation of Charles Evans.

That a former resident was called Evans could be indicative of the Shury/Evans family link, a notion strengthened by the profession attributed to Charles Evans in 1734 as a brewer.

The brothers Charles and John both lived in Stert Street, paying rates on separate properties in 1776 and still in 1785, the year their mother Elizabeth died. The first indication of Charles' criminal proclivities came in 1784, when he was fined £5 for poaching with guns. Then in 1785, as later evidence would show, he (and Giles Covington) robbed St Nicolas' Church, only a matter of days before his mother's funeral was held in the very same building!

By 1787 Charles was no longer a property owner in his own right, and was living in one of John's houses. It was nonetheless another substantial property in Stert Street, and the next year Charles achieved a certain status by acquiring a Berkshire Game Certificate in October and a licence to run an alehouse in September (endorsed, in his official capacity, by Roger Covington). This was The Chequer Inn in East St Helen's Street, the pub which featured so large in the crime spree of late 1789 – a fact which was no doubt of subsequent embarrassment to John, since the property was registered in his name.

The exact relationship between John and Charles can only be guessed at. Was Charles overawed by his more able older brother? Did he resent John's success, and resort to desperate means to try to emulate it? Or was he simply a profligate and selfish character, just a little too fond of the liquor that his family both produced and sold? John seems to have tried his best to give Charles a helping hand by letting him run The Chequer. Charles seems to have shown little gratitude, as demonstrated by Kilby's otherwise irrelevant anecdote about when 'they happened to take a game cock of Shury's brother's among the rest, which used to be out at different walks'. Unabashed, Charles (plausibly, on the evidence of the other direct quotes we have of him) said, ' "Never mind it, my boys. Take his head and feet off" ' to prevent a mark's being known in case it should be seen before it was boiled.' How betrayed John must have felt too when he learned that the theft of the St Nicolas' Church plate in 1785, for which he, as Churchwarden, had publicised a reward, had been committed by his very own younger brother!

John Shury's name occurs frequently in the various lists of Abingdon citizens who either voted or paid property or poor rates in the late eighteenth century. In 1796 he was named as one of Abingdon's major brewers in the Universal British Directory. He owned or leased numerous properties at this time, including The Oxford Arms in the market place, five separate properties on Stert Street, including a house, malthouse, brewery and stock, three tenements, a stable, another house, and some obviously sizeable 'vaults' (presumably for wine or beer) on which rates had been paid since at least 1776. When he died in January 1804 (StN) he was described in the press as an eminent brewer, but as a farmer in the church records, presumably in reference to the two acres of arable land that he acquired in Sutton Courtenay in 1789.

Smith, Thomas 'Oxford Tom': (? –1790) Like many men operating on the wrong side of the Georgian law, Thomas Smith, the horse thief whose confession would bring disaster to Shury and his confederates, had several aliases. Thomas Davis was one often applied, but he was most frequently referred to simply as Oxford Tom, both by the press and by those who knew him. His true name was Thomas Smith – at least that is what Daniel Harris always called him, and Harris, the young, energetic Prison Governor with the common touch, probably knew if anyone did. The name suggests he was from Oxford, or at least had frequent dealings there, so Harris was probably fairly reliably informed. Smith too was the name which appeared on the Assize record of the trial for the crime in which Shury would rue his involvement, 'for stealing a bay mare valued £20, goods of Simon Peck of Culham' on 14 November 1789. *Jackson's* reported his arrest and confinement at New Prison, Clerkenwell on 12 December 1789.

He was brought from New Gaol, Southwark on 1 March 1790 and found guilty at the Oxford Assizes of 4 March. He confessed to the Prison Chaplain on 21 March, the day before his execution. The long, irregular delay suggests that some plea-bargaining was going on. Eventually the authorities got what they wanted, even if Smith did not. Only his pronouncements on the thefts of Parson Nichols' and

Simon Peck's horses survive. But they are the essential ones as far as this history is concerned: the two in which Shury was integral.

Smith was probably a popular figure. Many men found guilty of theft in that century became heroes of the people if they could appeal to the sympathies of the downtrodden. The 'gallows speech' was something which had come to be expected, the behaviour of a condemned person being all part of the entertainment. It was also a gauge of guilt which was rather more persuasive to many than all the wordy deliberations of pro-establishment judges. In Smith's case there was little doubt about his culpability; it was the extent of his penitence that was being measured. *Jackson's* of 27 March 1790 reported:

> On Monday last Thomas Davis, alias Smith, alias Oxford Tom, was executed here … for stealing a mare from Culham, in this county. The gallows on which he suffered was about 50 feet high, erected upon the tower over the entrance to the Castle, and upon a drop constructed for that purpose. From this eminence he exhorted the spectators, who were very numerous, to be warned by his ignominious death, and assured them that from honest industry they might live much happier upon bread and water, than he had experienced for some years with an hundred guineas in his pocket.
>
> From the time of his conviction he manifested a desire to make some retaliation for his wicked course of life by discoveries that may prove beneficial, and by giving every information in his power to divers persons who daily applied in order to recover horses which had been stolen, and at the last he met his sentence with manly fortitude; yet his deportment was in every respect decent. In ascending the scaffold he rested a while at each landing place, and prayed most fervently for some minutes, but did not acknowledge the having himself stolen horses for some years past; but confessed the carrying on a most iniquitous trade of receiving them when stolen, and conveying them to distant parts for sale.

Shury was not the only one to suffer the consequences of Smith's confessions. *Jackson's* of 3 April 1790 mentions the recovery near Lewes in

Sussex of a horse belonging to Mr Thomas Juggins of Wheatley 'in consequence of information received from Smith, alias Oxford Tom'. The paper, hoping no doubt to inspire other gentlemen victims to take similar measures, praised the active role played by Juggins (and also by Simon Peck in the arrest of Oxford Tom himself) for their 'laudable spirit, almost regardless of either fatigue or expense'.

The discovery of another of Oxford Tom's accomplices, James Williams (1760?–1790), was noted in *Jackson's* of 15 May 1790. Williams had been Juggins' servant, and was discovered, 'in the thieves' phrase, *at home*, being in Clerkenwell prison for stealing a saddle'. Williams was taken to Oxford at the end of June, where he found himself in company with Shury and Castle. All three were tried at the same Assizes, and for his part in stealing Juggins' brown mare and black gelding, Williams received the death penalty. As with Smith, his execution was delayed beyond the following Monday (when Castle and Shury duly met their ends), and it was not until Monday 2 August that the sentence was carried out, despite Williams' continuing protestations of innocence.

Spicer, Susannah (née Mazey): A woman whose evidence was significant because, whereas the other testimonies to John Castle's loose tongue had up to that time come exclusively from either bargemen or their families, the Spicers were a well-established family from the town itself. Susannah married David Spicer in 1762 (StH), and the couple had four children (three of whom died young) between 1762 and 1770 (StH), and another in 1777 (StN). Lawrence Spicer, possibly David's father, was a freeman and currier (i.e. a leather worker), paying rates from the 1750s to 1770s on what was obviously a substantial property in Stert Street. From 1766 to 1774, it is David Spicer's name which appears in the lists of local electors, and he who is named as the occupant of their home in August 1781. It seems from his association with the shadowy William Pratt that, freeman or no, Lawrence Spicer was yet another Abingdon man unable to keep his hands off other people's property. David may not have been totally free from such urges himself: in the summer of 1781 a warrant was issued to enable the Borough's constables to search his premises for two copper tea kettles he was suspected of having stolen.

Tramplett, Benjamin: (1741?–1816) Although he was a relatively minor victim of the crime spree of late 1789, Tramplett was probably the best known, being the proprietor of two of Abingdon's most prestigious public houses, The Crown & Thistle and The White Hart. Tramplett married in 1776 (StH) and had seven children between 1777 and 1795. It was The White Hart from where Kilby and Covington stole the five blankets and two suits one night in October 1789. Tramplett must have suspected them of rather more than just that, though, to think it worth while to make a special journey to Reading when Kilby was arrested.

Whitehead, George: (1732?–1812) Called 'bargeman to Mr Gleed' when interviewed in 1790, he married Martha in 1761 (s) and was buried aged 80 in 1812, having become a shoemaker in his later years (s).

Willoughby, Sir Christopher: (1749?–1808) The Justice of the Peace most involved in the Charteris case lived at Marsh Baldon House, about three miles from the scene of the murder and one mile from Toot Baldon, the village where Charteris lived. It is the correspondence and notes retained by Willoughby, and held now at the Oxfordshire Record Office, which provide the archive information central to this story.

Willoughby had leased Marsh Baldon House since 1754, and had purchased it by 1771, along with an estate of some 400 acres. Over the next few decades, a farmer at heart, he managed both to distinguish himself in numerous areas of public life and to build up a farm of model self-sufficiency.

As a JP, Willoughby's powers and functions gave him an insight into all aspects of country life. He had the authority to administer justice at Quarter or Petty Sessions, or even in his own home. He had an obligation to maintain the roads, bridges, prisons, and workhouses, supervised the licensing of public houses, levied rates, and controlled countless other aspects of county business. Yet, he probably had no designated staff, nor any effective administration, for that would have meant levying a higher rate in order to pay for it – something the wealthy were generally unwilling to contemplate, preferring an inefficient local government to an expensive one!

Willoughby appears to have undertaken his numerous magisterial responsibilities with diligence, but the pages of *Jackson's* show that he involved himself in much besides, most notably in the formative stages of the Radcliffe Infirmary in Oxford from 1771 onwards, and in championing a memorial to John Howard, the prison reformer, in St Paul's Cathedral in 1791.

But Willoughby's main passion was for farming. Arthur Young visited him in 1807 when compiling his survey of agricultural practices in Oxfordshire, and called him 'an attentive and reflecting proprietor' who

> annually kills 80 sheep, by agreement with a neighbour, and he eats all his own beef. He keeps nineteen cows for butter, milk, cream, and cheese. A productive dove-house yields an ample supply of pigeons. His ponds (having a small stream through them, and being well attended) afford him carp, tench, and perch … Poultry of all sorts in great abundance. Game. His own wheat, oats, and hay; makes his own malt, and raises hops and poles.

There was also a 70-year-old orchard of nine acres, producing large quantities of cider from an apple called the broad-nosed pippin. Full of praise, Young concluded: 'All this forms a system of family plenty' which is 'not only pleasant but profitable'. And it needed to be plentiful: the extended family living at Marsh Baldon House at this time numbered 30 persons!

Willoughby married twice, first Juliana Burvill, a vicar's daughter from Bexley in Kent in 1776, who failed to survive the birth of their only child, Juliana, in May 1777. He remarried only after a considerable gap, taking Martha Evans of Harley Street in January 1789. Making up for lost time he had 12 children by his second wife, between 1792 and 1807, stopped from fathering more, perhaps, only by his death the following year, aged 59. *Jackson's* of 6 February 1808 was fulsome in its praise, noting in particular that his 'abilities as Chairman of the Quarter Sessions for upwards of 20 years were so conspicuous as to render it unnecessary to attempt a panegyric'. He was made a baronet in 1794.

Woolsgrove, Benjamin: A man who owes his fleeting historical commemoration purely to his drinking habits, his alibi having been the friends he drank with in a number of Abingdon pubs on the evening of the Fair. He could have been either the Benjamin described as 'of Toot Baldon' who married Sarah Morris in 1757 (MB), and was granted legal settlement there in 1762, or his son (a twin) who was christened in 1768 (N). Likewise, it is not clear if it was the older or younger Ben who was buried in 1799 (TB).

Wright, Sir Sampson: (?–1792): The chief magistrate at Bow Street from 1780 to his death in 1792 was the man to whom Christopher Willoughby wrote when it became apparent that Covington was in London. In December 1789, Wright and two others had been 'appointed by the Lords of the Admiralty in the commission for examining and committing persons for trial who are or may be guilty of any piratical practices, coming within the jurisdiction of the High Court of Admiralty', according to *Jackson's* of 26 December 1789. With contacts made in this role, Wright was as likely as anyone to persuade the possessive Navy to release its grip on a valuable asset like Covington. He had been knighted in 1782.

APPENDIX 2:

Places and topics in the text

-+->-<-+-

Abingdon. Now in Oxfordshire, Abingdon lay in Berkshire at the time of the murder, and was the county town until the 1860s. The population of the town was 4,356 according to the census of March 1801. Of this number, the parish of St Helen's contained 3,836 people (1,759 males and 2,077 females) comprising 938 families in 799 houses. St Nicholas' Parish contained only 520 people, making a total Abingdon population of 4,356. One can assume a population of about 4,000 in the late 1780s, therefore.

Cloth-making flourished in Berkshire in the fourteenth and fifteenth centuries, and Reading and Abingdon, with the Thames providing a supply of water and a means of transportation, became centres of this industry. As a result, the weaving and spinning of hemp and flax were commonplace in Abingdon by the eighteenth century, and the occupation of 'sack-weaver' or 'hemp-dresser' a common one at the time of this history. Proximity to river water was also key to Abingdon's other main industry (and another with a strong influence on this story): malting and brewing, a tradition which followed the lead of the town's famous Abbey.

Abingdon Michaelmas Fair. Due to the influence of the Abbey, Abingdon once had more fairs than any other Berkshire town. The origin of the Michaelmas Fair can be traced back to the shortage of labour after the Black Death of 1349. Subsequently the local Justices of the Peace were authorised to fix the rates of wages, and these were proclaimed annually in various towns at Michaelmas. In Abingdon this meant the Monday before 11 October. On that day people would come from far and wide to learn the new rates of pay, and enter into contracts for the following year. On the next Monday a secondary fair was held. This came to be called the 'Runaways Fair', where people who had either failed to find employment or who had found it not to their satisfaction in the preceding seven days were given a second opportunity. Both fairs continue to this day.

An idea of the wide appeal of the Michaelmas Hiring Fair is given in *Jackson's* of 12 October 1805, when the paper claimed that 10,000 people attended. This seems a considerable overestimate, but judging by the entertainment available, it did no doubt attract huge numbers. On show were the alluring prospects of 'the beauty of the *Grand Turk's Palace*, the wonderful feats of *The Little Strong Woman*, and the *harmony* of the *Pentonville Organ*', a troop of equestrians, some German musicians, and a menagerie of wild beasts. Among the latter was a monkey. When a young farmer's 'enamorata' offered it a nut,

> the ungrateful animal bit her fingers severely; this so enraged her lover
> that he immediately seized poor pug by the tail, and would have dashed
> his brains out, but the nimble African sprung at him, and with his paws
> lacerated his face in a dreadful manner.

Another farcical scene concerned a woman whose bonnet was accidentally pulled off, 'bringing with it her cap and false hair, and exposing her bald pate, to the great amusement of the company'.

Wherever crowds gathered, pickpockets were sure to follow. The same article noted the robberies of 'a poor woman of about forty shillings, a countryman of about three pounds, and a farmer of his pocket book, containing notes to a considerable amount'. This rather implies that Charteris might not have been alone in carrying large amounts of cash at such events. He was not alone in meeting his doom on the day of the Fair either. According to *Jackson's* of 13 October 1781, 'a person standing near the Market House was unhappily killed by a stone which happened to fall from the top of the building, and striking his head, dashed out his brains, and killed him dead upon the spot'.

Alcohol. The confessions of Kilby and 'Oxford Tom' Smith reveal that most of their crimes occurred after drinking sessions, but also that enough were sufficiently premeditated to suggest that inebriation could not be considered the catalyst. The consumption of alcohol in eighteenth-century England was in any case commonplace as it was much less likely to be contaminated than water. Tea was just beginning to assert itself as the nation's staple beverage, but in rural areas beer remained the drink of choice. Indeed, ale was commonly provided to agricultural labourers as part of their daily wage, for instance, and even given to children as a safer alternative to impure water. In a town like Abingdon, with its multiplicity of breweries and public houses, mild inebriation was presumably therefore pretty much a normal state of being!

A licensing law of 1552 drew a distinction between alehouses, which brewed and sold beer on the premises; taverns, which sold wine in addition; and inns, which provided lodgings and stabling as well as food and drink. The Abingdon Borough authorities limited the number of annual licences for all such victuallers to 50 in 1731, but beer is easily brewed, and there are several references to unlicensed premises within this history. Alehouses were viewed with suspicion as places where the seeds of social dissent might flourish. A Quarter Sessions ruling for both Berkshire and Oxfordshire was published in *Jackson's* on 28 July 1787. To renew their licences Berkshire alehouse keepers were obliged to produce 'certificates of good fame, sober life and conversation', and constables and other peace officers were empowered to visit public houses on a regular basis, 'more particularly on the Lord's Day, commonly called Sunday, during the time of divine service, in order better to suppress all gaming, drunkenness, Sabbath breaking, and other licentious behaviour'. Given this, it is no surprise to find in *Jackson's* report on the horse theft with which Henry 'Cherry' Goodman had some connection in 1765 (see page 77) that when the culprits 'pleaded drunkenness as an excuse [they] had the misfortune to find that plea no extenuation of their offence'.

The same year, the Borough paid the Bellman Roger Covington

for 'drawing cry and fair copy for prohibiting unlicensed people selling ale (except at Fairs)'. This exemption is of particular relevance. Everyone who was questioned about their whereabouts on the day of the Fair spent time in one or more public houses; we can gather that they had ample opportunity to indulge elsewhere too!

Anatomy School. However antisocial their activities while alive, Castle, Covington, and Shury all made amends in some small way after their deaths, with unwitting contributions to eighteenth-century anatomical learning. An Act of 1751 ordered that the corpses of murderers could, if specified, be left suspended in chains in full view, as an example to others who might be tempted down the same unlawful path. The Act also specified that the execution should take place the next day but one following sentence, unless that should be a Sunday. With the Oxford Assizes normally on a Friday, most Oxford executions therefore took place on a Monday. Also contained in the Act was the stipulation that after conviction the prisoner was to be confined in a separate cell, and fed only bread and water, and that visitors could be admitted only with a licence. A clause of particular relevance, however, specifically ordered that the corpses should be anatomised, and that no burial should be permitted until after the dissection had taken place.

The gallows were virtually the only legitimate source of corpses for medical advancement, and even then the anatomists were often beaten to the bodies by people with a rather stronger moral claim: the friends or relatives of the deceased. This led to some unseemly scrambles, which no doubt added to the entertainment value of such occasions. Executions attracted huge numbers of spectators, but not everyone was there out of macabre curiosity. Some were there with the intention of claiming the body before the authorities could!

One of the earliest executions recorded in *Jackson's* was that of 17-year-old James Till in April 1754. He was executed at Green Ditch, in the fields to the north of Oxford. Here the public would have been almost within touching distance of the condemned man. A letter

from an unnamed University source printed in the paper the following week shows what precautions were necessary to ensure that Till's
body could be 'regularly delivered to the gentlemen of the University
for the purpose of anatomical lectures' without incident. To avoid the
reappearance of 'the rioters who carried away the bodies of the two
persons executed here about a month ago', Till's execution was
attended by 'several stout, resolute persons … with orders to lay hold
of, and secure in the Castle, any person or persons who should make
the least attempt towards carrying off the body'. The writer – a self-
interested anatomist himself, perhaps? – went on to suggest that
dissection should be

> extended to *all* malefactors in general, since, if the consigning of the
> bodies of murderers to this use may be expected to have a good influ-
> ence towards preventing murders, no reason can be assigned why the
> like good effects may not be expected from the like penalty annexed to
> other capital offences.

As Till himself had been found guilty only of stealing 70 guineas from
his master (capital offence though this was), it would in any case seem
that the anatomists had already taken the law into their own hands in
this respect. The letter-writer's logic was anyway questionable, since
the means by which the supporters of condemned men thwarted the
anatomists' intentions were often more gory than the results of any
surgeon's knife.

The execution of Isaac Darkin, alias Dumas, is a case in point.
There was an undoubted popular admiration for some criminals.
Anyone able to outwit authority and strike a blow for the common
man acquired a notoriety and popularity which even the conservative
press of the time felt unable to disguise. Highwaymen enjoyed a
particular romanticised popularity. Consequently when Darkin was
executed for a highway robbery at Nettlebed, *Jackson's* of 28 March
1761 recorded with open admiration that 'his behaviour in his last
moments was entirely correspondent to the steadiness of character
and intrepidity which he affected and maintained even in his most

dangerous enterprises'. Afterwards his body had been carried off 'in triumph' by bargemen, and 'most inhumanly mangled, in order (according to his request) to prevent his being anatomised'.

There was no such affray at the executions of Covington, Shury, or Castle. By then the science of anatomy had acquired a less ghoulish reputation with the establishment of a formal Anatomy School at Christ Church in 1766–7. Additionally, with Daniel Harris installed as the Prison Governor, the Castle walls had been largely rebuilt, both reducing the embarrassingly frequent escapes, and also enabling the authorities to conduct executions at a safe distance from the nearest spectator. A double execution in August 1787 – of Thomas White, for stealing silverware from Blenheim, and Charles Walter Wyatt, Post Master of Witney, for embezzlement – was the first to be conducted under this 'reformed mode'. The place of execution was 'over the intended Turnkey's Lodge, which forms part of the new boundary wall'; and only officials and other inmates were allowed within the walls. The ploy worked, and 'totally prevented that riot and disorder too often experienced on similar occasions'. Nonetheless, at 33 feet above the ground, the gallows were deliberately still plainly in public view.

So when the judge pronounced Shury and Castle guilty in July 1790, he was able to order 'their bodies to be delivered to the surgeons, to be dissected and anatomised' with greater confidence that this would in fact occur than would have been the case a few years earlier. After the execution, both bodies were left to hang in public view, and it was not until the afternoon that they

> were conveyed in a cart to the Anatomy School at Christ Church, where Dr Thomson, the Reader in Anatomy, next day gave a public lecture on the two bodies, to which the neighbouring faculty, as well as those of the place, were invited, together with the gentlemen of the University, and many of the principal inhabitants. The bodies were also publicly exhibited the day following.

Less than a year later, Covington's corpse provided Dr Christopher Pegge, another Reader in Anatomy, with a similar opportunity to enlighten the public.

The 1751 Act was amended in 1832. Although the corpse was still to be hung in chains, dissection was discontinued from that time, and the bodies buried in the prison precincts.

Bow Street Runners. The model for the modern police force was established in the mid-eighteenth century by the novelist Henry Fielding, followed on his death in 1754 by his blind half-brother, Sir John, who dispensed magisterial justice from their house in Bow Street, London. The capital had a particular need for organised law enforcement, as Henry Fielding, writing in 1751, showed:

> Whoever indeed considers the cities of London and Westminster with the late vast addition of their suburbs, the great irregularity of their buildings, the immense number of lanes, alleys, courts and by-places, must think that had they been intended for the very purpose of conceal-ment they could scarce have been better contrived. Upon such a view, the whole appears as a vast wood or forest in which a thief may harbour with as great a security as wild beasts do in the deserts of Africa or Arabia.

These scenes of urban chaos had obvious attractions as a place where a man-on-the-run like Covington might find anonymity among many others of the time. For a law-abiding citizen like his father, London had exerted an opposite force, encouraging him to settle in more peaceful surrounds. Giles was a fugitive from criminal justice in London, Roger a fugitive from its criminals! But things had changed since Roger's time. During the winter of 1789, exactly when Abingdon's stables, hen-roosts, and pigeon houses were being routinely emptied under Shury's malign influence, there was an alarming rise in violent robberies in London. This inspired Sir Samp-son Wright, the Bow Street magistrate who succeeded the Fieldings in 1782, to introduce an armed foot patrol from dusk to midnight in April 1790 – which, from the newly arrived Covington's point of view, was unfortunate timing. The idea of joining the Navy may therefore have occurred to him only once he had arrived in the capital, and realised that while he might have outwitted the volunteer constables of Abingdon, the Runners were a rather different proposition.

A Bow Street officer called Jealous was foremost in Covington's arrest, and it was probably therefore Jealous who happened in that 'highly providential' way to find the note in his pocket which linked Covington with the *HMS London*. Considering the demands closer to home, it is indicative of the influence of Willoughby that Jealous and a second officer could be spared to make the journey to Spithead near Portsmouth to arrest Covington, and then accompany him all the way to Oxford. It is also clear from this that Covington was considered an especially significant catch.

Constables. For most of the eighteenth century, the army was the only efficient force against serious public disorder. The Fielding brothers set a new trend when they established the Bow Street Runners, but elsewhere law enforcement was essentially still voluntary, depending on the services of local constables appointed on an annual basis, and paid for by local taxes. A major task was to escort vagrants out of the parish. Had her murderers not found her first, the pauper woman would no doubt have soon attracted the attentions of the Culham constables. Anyone in her position who might become a burden on the poor rate was driven unceremoniously from parish to parish, a short-sighted policy which reduced the mobility of labour and aggravated unemployment. But the constables also of course pursued criminals: the search for Castle and Covington involved paying £1 5s 3d to John Hinchin (or Kinchin), and 9s to two militia men for travelling to Abingdon, Watlington, and beyond. The cost of pursuing Kilby and Castle (again, his whereabouts being less predictable on account of the mobility of his profession on the river) was 18s, paid to Edward Bailey for nine days @ 2s a day and 12s to Edward Webb for six days. These costs were paid by the Oxfordshire authorities, but it is not clear which parish these constables actually represented.

The Fight At Banbury. The 'fight at Banbury' to which Kilby refers in his confession was an event of national importance, and no-one at the time could have mistaken what he was referring to. The main contest, between Johnson and Perrins, attracted 10,000 people, according to *Jackson's* of 24 October 1789. Indeed the numbers were so great that no sooner had Johnson arrived at noon on the 22nd than the crowd broke down the fence, at which time 'it was found expedient to throw open the doors and allow the populace to enter gratis' – which was bad luck on those one thousand people who had already paid half a guinea to enter. The fight was held on a turf stage about 40 feet in diameter, and began about one o'clock. Despite being the smaller man, Johnson won in 1 hour 13 minutes, enabling him, in the *Gazette's* account of 26 October, to pocket at least 250 guineas and name himself Champion of England.

More entertainment followed when Pickard, one of Perrins' seconds, accused Johnson of 'fighting like a coward'. Johnson's reaction was to challenge Pickard to an immediate contest for 100 guineas, 'but not relishing this specimen of his adversary's strength and agility, he judiciously declined'. Pickard did fancy his chances against 'George the Brewer' though, and fought a bloody bout with him the next day (23rd). The *Gazette* called this 'the most bloody conflict that was ever remembered upon any stage', observing that 'less humanity between man and man was absolutely impossible'. *Jackson's* was keen to point out that the 'principal men of science throughout the kingdom were present', but it is a comment which betrays a certain vested interest in the activity. Few citizens, rich or poor, educated or not, would deny a fascination with such contests, and the newspaper probably sold many additional copies to people who, with a certain timelessness, considered such 'sport' more newsworthy than the national and international politics which normally dominated its pages. The *Gazette*, indeed, devoted an extraordinary one and a half columns to the event. An unrestrained assembly of thousands of people, liable to be stirred to violence by the nature of the spectacle, was not something the authorities could ignore, however. So when, on 7 November,

Jackson's repeated the national news that a fight between Johnson and Big Ben (who himself had fought someone called Jacombs in a bout lasting 1 hour 25 minutes at Banbury) had been arranged, the implicit approval of the paper was not matched by that of the magistrates. The very next week, the Oxfordshire Clerk of the Peace published an order requiring constables to report 'any riotous assembly or tumultuous meeting for boxing, fighting or any other illegal purpose … or any stage erected for any such purpose'.

The repercussions of 'the Fight at Banbury' did not end there. *Jackson's* of 5 December 1789 noted that all the 'celebrated' principal protagonists, 'together with all the aiders and abettors of that tumultuous and illegal assembly, from the umpires to the bottle holders' were involved in a rather different contest, where none of them were favourites. Their opponents? The learned worthies of the King's Bench in London!

Big Ben was still at the forefront of his sport over a year later, when *Jackson's* of 12 February 1791 announced in breathless tones that 'Big Ben has a *twin brother*, as large as himself, with whom he has fought, at different times, regularly, ever since they were twelve years old. Each has beaten the other successively, and they have *loved* and *fought* each other into their present state.' One can imagine Covington, the 'excellent pugilist', getting a little thrill from this news, if it filtered down to him during his uncertain days awaiting trial. It is not clear if Covington had gone to the Fight at Banbury himself. Kilby was certainly there, and Shury was assuredly not the kind of man to miss such a momentous occasion. Quite possibly he, Kilby, and Smith met at the fight for the very first time; quite possibly they travelled back together, and planned the theft of Nichols' horse en route.

Judicial sentences. The late eighteenth and early nineteenth centuries saw a flowering of literature, architecture, and the arts, yet were characterised by the most callous treatment of prisoners and paupers in modern times. By the end of the eighteenth century some 200 offences were punishable by death, including crimes as trivial as the theft of a handkerchief. Such was the illogical chaos of the law that in theory it made no difference whether the owner of the handkerchief had been killed in the process, and as 'dead men tell no tales' the law in effect actually encouraged thieves to murder their victims!

But this was an age which was becoming more humane, and juries were often reluctant to convict men of minor offences that would lead them to the gallows. Even then, it is not as if Shury and his cohorts would have been ignorant of the risks entailed in their behaviour. Everyone, other perhaps than Covington, who would then have been only 16 years old, would have registered the fate of Edward Moor, who was sentenced at the Abingdon Quarter Sessions of October 1783 to seven years' transportation to Nova Scotia for 'petit larceny'. *Jackson's* called this 'the only instance of a sentence of transportation given in that corporation for near a century'.

The Abingdon Assizes of July 1788 would have given Shury and his companions cause for thought too. With the memory of the Charteris murder still fresh in their minds, all the men would have pondered the death sentences (commuted to transportation) meted out merely for sheep-stealing and house-breaking. Some other (Oxford) punishments recorded in *Jackson's* between 1788 and 1790 were:

– theft of clothes from the University: two years' hard labour at the Castle; theft of fowls: six months' hard labour; manslaughter: six months' hard labour (8 March 1788)

– theft of three ducks and a drake: two years at the House of Correction; assisting a youth to steal from his master's shop: seven years' transportation (5 April 1788)

– stealing lead: seven years' transportation; stealing £100: burnt in the hand and two years' hard labour (14 March 1789)

- stealing a sack of wheat and 2s ½d: two years and one year hard labour in the Castle respectively (16 January 1790)

- theft of a horse, a silver pint mug and a watch, and money: all seven years' transportation; stealing cotton and muslin, both one year in prison; stealing a shirt: one month in prison and whipped (6 March 1790)

- stealing clothes, and wool, and for an assault: all seven years' transportation (17 July 1790)

Despite such penalties, it is indicative of the desperate plight of the poor that opportunist thieves were everywhere. Kilby and Castle alone revealed more than a dozen culpable Abingdon men. Shury probably knew a very large number more. Many probably fell into the category described by the 4th Duke of Marlborough a few years later when responding to a survey published by Arthur Young in 1813 for the Board of Agriculture. With reference to poor men falling prey to temptation, Marlborough thought that 'this depravity originated in the inadequacy of wages to the support of themselves and families, which compel many, contrary to their inclination, to have recourse to dishonest means'. He continued:

> This very culpable conduct in the poor people, I am sorry to say, origi-
> nated chiefly in past ill treatment, as it is a fact which cannot be denied,
> that for many years past, poor men who had large families, have per-
> formed their labour with no better a subsistence than scarcely sufficient
> bread and water; the whole family of course must submit to the same
> humiliating fare. Such distress, I conceive, will be thought sufficient to
> pervert a natural good disposition.

Marlborough's enlightened assessment could be applied to Castle and Kilby, and maybe even to Covington as the youngest, possibly disowned, son. For Shury, however, there was no such excuse. And whatever the motivation, it would be difficult to match the audacity of the events at the Oxford Assizes of March 1787 when 'a gentleman upon the Grand Jury had his pocket picked in court; several others also lost their money, and one farmer his watch, by the dexterity of the light fingered gentry who attended'. This humorous admiration for the sheer temerity of the pickpockets is typical of *Jackson's* coverage of non-violent crimes of this sort. Often a pronouncement on the depravity of the times, or a warning to all honest citizens, would also be inserted, but it is often difficult to discern any *real* outrage. Then as now, crime was news, and news sold papers!

HMS London. The vessel on which Covington enlisted in May 1790 was one of the most important in the British fleet. 177 feet long by 50 wide, she had been one of 36 vessels assembled in a 'Grand Fleet' at Spithead in 1779 as a response to the increasing rebelliousness of the American colonies. In 1783, following action against the French in the Caribbean, and Britain's humiliating recognition of America's right to independence, the *London* returned to British waters.

1790 was a relatively quiet year in terms of the naval activity of the period. Britain had recovered from its ignominious American campaign, and was party to a series of diplomatic alliances. However, tensions with Spain were still apparent, especially in respect of mercantile rights on the Pacific north coast of America, and the strategically important outpost of Gibraltar. The *London* was a part of a fleet readied to meet that threat. Covington enlisted on 11 May. According to her log books, she left Chatham two days later, moored off Gillingham from 26 May to 9 June, arrived at Spithead on 8 July, then moored at Torbay from 29 July. It was here that the fleet assembled, and on 8 August the *London* set sail 'in company with Admiral Earl Howe with 31 sail of the line, 8 frigates, 2 fireships, 1 hospital ship and 3 cutters'. This fleet moored off the Lizard from 19 to 23 August, off Land's End 24 to 31 August, off Scilly and the Lizard from 1 to 14 September, and at Spithead from 15 September to 9 October. The *London* was accorded particular status in September as the flagship of Vice-Admiral Sir Alexander Hood under the command of William (later Sir William) Domett. Military action proved unnecessary, however, and the signing of a convention with Spain meant that the *London* remained moored at Spithead from 25 October to the end of the year, when the fleet was dismantled. From Covington's point of view it might have been better if the diplomatic manoeuvrings had failed, because it was only then, when the necessity for fully manned vessels had passed, that the civil authorities made their move to reclaim him.

If Covington ever felt he had truly eluded the civil authorities, he would have found himself frequently reminded of the rather more immediate justice of the sea. The ship's crew was split pretty much equally between able seamen, ordinary seamen, and inexperienced landsmen like Covington. For such men, conditions on board a naval ship – cramped, cold, and damp though they were – probably offered considerable advantages over life ashore. Certainly the diet was preferable, as seamen enjoyed the privilege of a hot dinner daily, with beef, bread, and cheese, and sometimes vegetables and fruit. Yet how Britain so successfully 'ruled the waves', with her seamen entitled to a gallon of beer per man per day, is a decided mystery. Afloat or ashore, mild inebriation was evidently the order of the Georgian day!

During Covington's time on board the *London*, the standard punishment for any misdemeanour was 12 or 24 lashes. He kept his nose clean – and indeed was an exemplary sailor – but other landsmen were less obliging, and there are frequent references in the logbook to floggings for dereliction, insolence, and quarrelling. For a seaman found guilty of theft, the punishment was different. Thieving was a serious breach of the mutual trust which was an essential element of any efficient crew. It was the crew, therefore, who were left to administer their own form of justice on 9 November as the seaman Thomas White was made to 'run the gauntlet three times around the deck'.

On 19 November came an event which, if it ever reached Covington's ears, might have made him wistful for home, and the wife and child he had been forced to abandon. On that day 'was delivered of a girl, Hannah Scott, the wife of Job Scott of 31 regiment'. Scott was a marine, one of the men whose presence at one point swelled the total numbers aboard the *London* to over 1,000. The birth is indicative of the relaxed nature of the shipboard routine when in port. Women, not necessarily always wives, were tolerated, and entertainments of various sorts allowed. On 7 December, the *London*'s log book noted that most officers and soldiers disembarked, and on the 21st a launch removed 'a number of our men that is discharged at their own request, to be paid at the Commissioner's office in the Yard'. Covington was not among them. He had made sufficiently good account of himself to be called a 'seaman' by now, in half the time normally expected, and was no doubt welcome to stay aboard.

A few days before his arrest, Covington probably had the strongest reminder yet of his own mortality when the *London* received four prisoners from another ship, the *Royal William*, on 22 December. One man was classed as insane, one still to be tried, a seaman called Richard Fox was under sentence of 100 lashes, but the fourth man, Francis Underhill, was facing the death penalty (usually applied only for murder and buggery). Covington was in Oxford Goal by the time the last two received their punishments, the Navy having relinquished him on 2 January 1791, to the satisfaction of neither. Covington knew what fate awaited him, and the Navy knew when it had lost a good man! He had been ever-present in the London's muster lists, appearing always as Number 138. His final logbook reference comes on 19 January, when the arrears of his wages were paid off.

The *London* saw service in the Napoleonic wars, and was broken up in 1811.

Militia. As chance had it, Kilby was required to report for Militia duty very soon after he became wanted by the authorities. The Berkshire regiment's annual month of training, always held at either Reading or Newbury, was announced in a notice dated 25 March 1790. It was to commence with an inspection on Monday 10 May by Lord Craven, Lord Lieutenant of Berkshire, to be held in Reading Marketplace. 28 days' training would follow, and failure to report would be treated as desertion. This was the initial charge levelled at Kilby when he was captured. Despite penalties of six months in prison or a £20 fine, there would inevitably be one or two such cases every year.

Indeed some men made a career out of desertion, knowing that if they could remain undetected for the duration of the 28 days of training, there was seemingly little chance of being called to book. Pride of place in this respect must go to Thomas Hodgson of Wantage. When he was executed in 1787 in Ipswich for robbery, according to Emma Thoyts 1897 history of the regiment, he claimed to have enlisted in English, Irish, and Scottish regiments under 49 different names, sometimes even with different recruiting parties of the same regiment, but seldom staying longer than a day. By this means – even though he was only 26 when executed – he had acquired 397 guineas in bounty money, but been convicted only three times. And this despite a reward of 20s for anyone turning over a Militia deserter, and a penalty of £5 imposed on anyone found guilty of harbouring one.

The Berkshire Militia had a longer consecutive history than any other regiment, having been recognised from 1640 onwards. It was one of the first regiments to be embodied as a response to the threat of invasion by France in 1757, and had little difficulty in supplying its quota – fixed at 560 men (of at least 5'4" in height) out of the 32,000 required from the whole country by 1786. Every parish was expected to contribute to this county quota, and was fined for any shortfall.

Nuneham Park and House. As Charteris' body was found in Nuneham parish, and the estate of the aristocratic Harcourt family virtually *was* the parish, the stile on which he met his doom must have been on the very edge of their estate. An 1802 map of Culham parish (held at the Oxfordshire Record Office) names these adjacent fields of Culham Mead (see map on page xi). Assuming that these had remained unaltered in the preceding 15 years, there are two possibilities for the precise location of the murder. The last independent sighting of Charteris (John King at the trial) was 'in the second ground beyond

'View of Nuneham from the Wood' published by John and Josiah Boydell in 1794. The wide track and numerous pedestrians suggest that access was relatively easy. Lawns run down to the Thames from the House, much as today. *(Photo: Mark Davies)*

Culham Mead in 2002, looking east along the southern bank of the Thames. In essence, the scenery has probably altered little in 200 years, the open grassland of the Mead, the distant woods of Nuneham Park, and the ridge of Culham Heath remaining much as they would have appeared to Charteris on his last walk homewards. (*Photo: Mark Davies*)

the Water Turnpike'. *Jackson's* called this Ditch End, but the 1802 map identifies it either as Farther Copse or Wick Meadow. Kilby said the gang overtook Charteris 'at the stile within one ground of Newnham Wood'. Although some public access was tolerated, it seems unlikely that Charteris intended crossing Harcourt's land, with the uninviting prospect of walking through Lock Wood in the gathering gloom. His shortest route would have been to walk along the river bank, in which case it was probably the stile between Baker's Ground and Wood End Sideling on which he was killed. Alternatively he might have intended to skirt the wood on the opposite side by walking along the riding which marked the edge of the Harcourt estate, then taking the lane which ran towards the road to Oxford and his home village of Toot Baldon beyond. In this case, a stile where three fields – Wood End, Forty Acres, and Brook's Close – met a little upslope from the river might be the spot. Wherever it was, the railway must now run very close.

Unless he had special privileges, it would have been highly inadvisable for Charteris to trespass on Harcourt's land anyway, judging by the regular warnings printed in *Jackson's*. The Abingdon horse races, held on the adjacent grassland of Culham Heath (until 1811), were times of particular concern, prompting this typical notice in *Jackson's* in September 1775, for instance:

> No person will be permitted to go through Nuneham Park to Abingdon Races on Culham Heath, as it has been attended with many inconveniences from the improper use that has been made of that privilege for some years past, by the foot-people getting over, pulling off, and breaking the park pales, to the great detriment of the plantations; as well as horse-people riding over and greatly damaging the turf, and also the great number of carriages damaging the road when the weather proves wet.

Similar notices appeared whenever the races were held for the remainder of the century.

The 1st Earl Harcourt, Simon, died in September 1777, a few

months after the trespass by the party of bargemen which included Henry Goodman and T. Hewitt (see Goodman). This was not the last such incident, if the notices published by the 2nd Earl, George Simon, in 1779 and 1780 are any guide. These prohibited the

> towing of barges up the river higher than the corner of the wood, and the Rod Aight by Nuneham Lock, persons coming into the Park under various pretences, or passing through the same without permission, others landing in places up the river within the said Park and Manor.

In addition 'all communication from the river to the House will be for the future entirely stopped, by gardens that are now making, unless to those who *previously* apply to the gardener for permission'. Finally it warned those who *were* given leave to enter 'to bring no dogs with them, as the keepers have orders to shoot all such as are found therein'. By 1780 no-one, no matter what their business or credentials, was permitted to cross the grounds during the races, and by the time of a notice in *Jackson's* of 14 September 1782 even 'gentlemen with tickets and keys' were prohibited entry. To underline the point, the estate's widely famed 'pleasure ground and gardens' were closed too. These grounds, incorporating the designs of Capability Brown, were described by William Combe in 1794 as 'a superb domain, containing near twelve hundred acres … Beyond the lawns it assumes a more wild and forest appearance, while its skirts, where thick woods do not intervene, offer prospects which, in different parts, have contrasted charms of distance, grandeur and beauty.'

Public houses in Abingdon. The following pubs (none of which survive under the same name) are all mentioned in the documents retained by Christopher Willoughby, and held at the Oxfordshire Record Office. Much of the information derives from *Inns and Ale-houses of Abingdon 1550–1978* by Jacqueline Smith and John Carter.

BLACK HORSE – one of the pubs visited on the day of the Fair by an unnamed interviewee. It is noted as being somewhere in Stert Street between 1831 and 1859.

CHEQUER INN – run by Shury from at least 30 September 1788 (when he was granted a licence) to at least November 1789, when it was the nerve centre of the gang's activities. The Chequer's approximate location is revealed in the Borough Minutes for 5 June 1795, when reference is made to 'a mound between the Chequer and Mr Thomas Crapper's premises in East St Helen's Street'.

DROPSHORTS – Kilby mentioned 'a house in Sutton called Dropshorts where they sell liquor without any licence' when recounting the theft of Mr Nichols' horse in October 1789.

FIGHTING COCKS – stood next to The Crown & Thistle in Bridge Street and was later incorporated into this more famous establishment. The name was retained as part of Burford House, which was in the occupation of Mr Edward Child (whose Abbey Brewery was later absorbed into Abingdon's longest surviving brewery of Morland's) according to the Borough Minutes of 24 February 1789. 'Burford' is one of the alternative names applied to Abingdon Bridge (White Hart Bridge being another – see below), and derives from the 'borough ford' which preceded the mediaeval construction.

HALF MOON – stood on the western side of the southern end of East St Helen's Street, facing the wharves, and was therefore a convenient local for someone like Peter Pickman with nearby business interests. The landlord, according to a notice in *Jackson's* of 20 December 1788, was William Lawrence, who announced that a pony, saddle, and bridle left at the pub by two men a week earlier would be sold to meet their undischarged reckoning.

MAGPYE – Betsy Crawford was the landlady in 1790, and still in 1796, when the pub is accorded the status of a mention in the Universal British Directory and its landlady the status of 'Mrs Elizabeth Crawford'.

OXFORD ARMS – a notice in *Jackson's* places the Oxford Arms in the Market Place in 1781. Thomas Giles had been the proprietor in 1771, according to the Poor Rate rolls, and still in 1789, as Kilby names him as the landlord when describing the theft of Nichols' horse in October 1789. Giles was still the proprietor of both The Oxford Arms and The Town Sergeant in 1796, according to the Universal British Directory – the latter name deriving from Giles' civic role.

SHIP – apart from two references, one by Benjamin Woolsgrove and one by an unnamed person who had also been at the Fair on the day of the murder, nothing is known about this establishment.

WHARF HOUSE – this was referred to by two people at the Fair, and although not necessarily a drinking establishment, it was likely to be part of the complex of riverside buildings at 58/70 East St Helen's Street which was leased to Peter Pickman by William Tomkins.

WHITE HART – James Powell, already the landlord of the smaller The Crown & Thistle on the opposite side of Bridge Street, first took the lease in 1755, and ran it till his retirement 21 years later, when a notice in *Jackson*'s emphasised the inn's 'exceedingly pleasant and spacious garden, lying close by the river side, well laid out in walks, and planted'. The next year the lease was taken by Benjamin Tramplett, who remained until 1793. Powell still owned the property at his death early in 1797 at the age of 70. The pub was demolished in order to build a new gaol in 1806 (designed by the ubiquitous Oxford Gaoler Daniel Harris). There are two references in Kilby's confessions to crossing the 'hard' bridge. This obviously derives from the White Hart, and was either a colloquial name, or an indication of Kilby's uneducated accent!

St Helen's Church, Abingdon. Known as 'the people's church', St Helen's served the townspeople, merchants and professional classes of Abingdon. The majority of personalities featured in this book worshipped there.

St Nic(h)olas' Church, Abingdon. Originally the church of the lay servants and tenants of Abingdon Abbey, by the eighteenth century St Nicolas' tended to be favoured by Abingdon's wealthy elite, which included the Shury family. The Stert Stream was covered over under Abingdon's first Paving Act of 1794, but still runs beneath the nave of the church. One of the crimes Covington allegedly admitted to was the theft of three items of silverware – a flagon, plate and paten – plus a gilt cup or chalice from the church. The crime was noted in *Jackson's* of 3 September 1785, public proclamations were made in and around Abingdon and Oxford, and handbills printed for distribution locally and in London. In addition an advert was placed in the local papers, announcing a reward of 20 guineas, to be paid by the Churchwarden, Mr John Shury. Later evidence suggests that Shury need not have looked very far, as it was his own brother Charles who, along with Covington, committed the audacious crime. A replacement set of silverware was provided by a wealthy parishioner in 1786.

Scotchman. Although Charteris was described as 'Scotch' in the reward notice printed in *Jackson's* of 13 October 1787, this was probably an error, caused by initial confusion over his profession. Charteris is certainly a name suggesting Scottish origins, but 'Scotchman' was also a generic term used to describe a petty trader at this time. The Oxford English Dictionary defines the term as 'a travelling draper or pedlar' or 'an itinerant trader of household goods on credit'. The origin of the term might therefore be linked with the old English use of 'scotch', commonly used in Berkshire, meaning to score, or in this context, keep a tally of customers' credit (*Glossary of Berkshire Words and Phrases* by B. Lowsley, English Dialect Society, 1888).

It is unlikely that the money for which he was murdered was acquired by Charteris on the day of the Fair. Kilby's confession implies that Shury was not alone in knowing that he often carried money on his person, and while that in itself constituted an obvious risk, country tradesmen probably had few other options. There is every indication that Charteris lived alone, so leaving large sums at home would have comprised an equal risk in these lawless times. Forty guineas was an enormous sum, though. By comparison, the returns made to the Board of Agriculture in 1790 (reproduced in Arthur Young's 1813 survey) put the typical wages of Oxfordshire labourers at 6s 6d per week in winter, 9s in summer, and 13s during harvest.

Charteris was therefore carrying with him the equivalent of about two years' income! The temptation to give evidence leading to the arrest of the murderers, and earn the identical amount, must have been alluring to many.

Swift Ditch. The branch of the Thames on which the Waterturnpike House and adjacent lock stood was the river's main navigation in 1787, and had been since at least 1632. That is the year that John Taylor's book *Thame Isis* observed that the Swift Ditch was preferred to the longer route past Abingdon town, which was impeded by numerous shallows and ferries and the low arches of the town's medieval bridge. Swift Ditch was a means of avoiding these hazards. It was entered less than a mile downstream of Nuneham Park, and ran for nearly two miles along the south eastern edge of Andersey Island to join today's main course of the Thames at Culham Bridge, where the pauper woman met her death. It shows the importance of the route that one of the first three pound locks ever built on the Thames was located here. The lock was completed at some point between 1624 and 1638, and lay about a hundred yards along the stream. Another 500 yards or so downstream there lay a second barrier, a single-gated flashlock, giving rise to the names of two of the adjacent meadows – Old Lock Ground and Old Lock Meadow – in the 1802 map of Culham parish (see page xi).

Even Swift Ditch was not without its drawbacks, however. *Jackson's* of 25 Feb 1764 stated that when the first barges to leave Oxford

> since the late extensive rains first swelled the flood ... in the cut called the Old Ditch, above Culham Bridge, they found themselves aground, notwithstanding the country round these parts appears to have water in too great plenty; for the vast and long continued torrent has carried down a great quantity of soil which had rested there, and obliged them to lighten their vessels to get over it.

By-passed by Swift Ditch, Abingdon's traders had an obvious incentive to encourage access to the town's wharves, so Abingdon Lock was

'Culham Bridge', published by Samuel Ireland in 1792. This is where the pauper woman met her death, at the confluence of Swift Ditch with the branch of the Thames passing Abingdon. St Helen's spire is in the distance.

Swift Ditch Lock in 2002 – the stonework, probably dating from 1783, still 'firm and exact laid', as Fred Thacker wrote in 1910. (*Photo: Mark Davies*)

built near the Abbey in 1790, the river deepened, and a new naviga-tion arch added to Abingdon Bridge. This was one example of the extensive improvements occurring on the Thames at this time, as a response to the much increased river traffic deriving from Britain's ever-expanding canal network. Two canals were of particular rele-vance to Oxford and Abingdon. The Thames and Severn Canal (completed 1789) opened up a route to the upper Thames from Stroud in Gloucestershire (and thereby also the Severn ports of South Wales) and the Oxford Canal (completed in 1790) placed Oxford briefly on the shortest navigable route between the newly industrial-ising Midlands and London. In the Oxford area, the Governor of the Castle Gaol, Daniel Harris, was central to both the completion of the Canal and improvements on the river.

Once Abingdon Lock was opened early in 1791, Swift Ditch fell rapidly into disuse. So when Samuel Ireland passed this way a year or so before the publication of his 1792 *Picturesque Views on the River Thames*, he observed that:

> Within about a mile of the town of Abingdon, a new cut is formed for the convenience of the navigation, which has rendered the old stream towards Culham bridge entirely useless; this cut has not only shortened the distance towards Abingdon very considerably, but is become necessary from the shallowness of the stream, which in dry seasons has not sufficient water for the purposes of navigation.

Ireland was writing from experience: to reach Abingdon, he had to have his boat dragged over Abingdon Lock, so shallow was the Thames at that point. Afloat again, he observed 'a handsome wharf is lately completed at the extremity of the town of Abingdon, beyond which a new cut, forming a small curve, joins the main river a little below Culham bridge.' Ireland was wrong in thinking the river's route through Abingdon artificial, but the comment reveals the novelty implicit in taking a vessel this way.

Waterturnpike House and Lock. According to the Convocation Accounts of Abingdon Abbey noted in Fred Thacker's first volume of *The Thames Highway* (1914), two houses were built alongside the lock on Swift Ditch in the mid-seventeenth century. In 1647 £105 was paid 'for repair of the turnpike at Swift Ditch and for the building of the house there' and in 1652 another building, a two-roomed cottage, was built 'upon the wall of the southside of the turnpike at Swift Ditch'. At this time, the lock-keeper was required to be a single man and was forbidden to sell alcohol or victuals. This prohibition may have continued through to the next century, one rationale for having two dwelling places being that the resident of one would derive a living from the tolls on the boats, the other from retailing alcohol and provisions. It was the tolls which gave rise to the Waterturnpike name. As with the turnpike roads, where the tolls levied on traffic paid for maintenance, the same concept applied on the river, where passing barges would be charged as a means of keeping the navigation in repair.

Major improvements to the lock were undertaken in 1783. *Jackson's* of 7 June 1783 carried an invitation to tender for 'taking down and rebuilding the Old Lock at Culham … and likewise for repairing the walls above the said lock'. The work was soon underway, *Jackson's* of 19 July 1783 stating that 'no boat or boats will be permitted to pass through … and that no water is to be drawn at any of the turnpike gates above or below the said lock till further notice'. A year later the Commissioners of Sewers advertised that 'the tolls and duties arising at Culham Turnpikes and the Old Lock' were to be let 'to the best bidder, for one year, from 10th October'. The notice added that 'the shutting tackle at the Old Lock and sluices at Culham Turnpikes is to be kept in repair by the tenant.' In 1785 this tenant was a man called Collins, related no doubt to the Abingdon bargemasters of that name, who paid £46 for a year's rent. It is not clear if he actually resided there, but someone who definitely did was Thomas Hewitt. He paid the Commissioners a mere £2 a year in rent, and whatever else his role there entailed, he was acting as publican on the evening of the Fair.

By the end of 1790, with the preferred route soon to pass Abingdon itself via the new Abingdon Lock near the Abbey, the boats and tackle at the Swift Ditch lock were removed and the gates locked. Thomas Hewitt must have suffered from the instant reduction in trade, as in May 1792 the Thames Commissioners threatened him with eviction from the house at what was then described as 'Cullum Old Lock' for falling behind with his rent. At the same time Henry Collins paid £14 3s 4d for part of a year's rent for the lock and pound, presumably solely for the purpose of mooring and maintaining his family's fleet of barges.

Hewitt was still 'the tenant of the house at Cullham old lock' in August 1798, when he was again behind with his rent to the tune of £8, or four years. Stubbornly he refused to move out when the house was sold for £24 10s in June 1799, and it needed the efforts of a bailiff finally to eject him in the August of that year. Soon after, 'the house being totally useless to the Commissioners', as Thacker put it in the 1920 second volume of *The Thames Highway* (and from which most of the information above is taken), it was demolished.

In 1857 the site reverted to the Lord of Culham Manor, then James Morrell, the Oxford brewer. That year the Commissioners sold him 'the old Turnpike or Pound Lock and site upon which a cottage formerly stood situate on the back stream or river at Culham', according to Thacker, who found occasion to explore Swift Ditch in 1910. At that time he found:

> For the most part the course is winding and narrow; thickly grown up
> and overhung with a jungle of plants and hedges and lofty timber that
> almost shut out the sunlight from its quiet flow. But here and there the
> course is wide and deep, as no doubt it was throughout, when first re-
> opened nearly three centuries ago.

He commented also on the lock chamber, about 28 feet in width and 75 to 80 feet long, with walls of 'firm and exact stonework, beautifully laid' along with 'beautiful and unsuspected pools'. One of the pools was above the lock 'with accommodation for a whole fleet of barges, and another below, still larger', comprising in all 'a revelation of much Thames beauty almost undreamed of'. Elements of Thacker's 1910 description hold true today; elements were no doubt true a century and a quarter earlier, when Charteris undertook his fatal walk home.

Sources and further reading

->->-<-<-

BABBINGTON, Anthony   *A House In Bow Street*, Barry Rose, 1999

BOARDMAN, Carl   *Oxfordshire Sinners and Villains*,
Alan Sutton, 1994

COMBE, William   *An History of the River Thames*, John & Josiah
Boydell, 1794

COX, Mieneke   *Abingdon: an 18th Century Town*, self-published,
1999

DAVIES, Mark
& ROBINSON, Catherine   *A Towpath Walk In Oxford*, Oxford Towpath
Press, 2001

HAMBLETON, Michael   *The Story of the Abingdon Baptist Church
1649–2000*, Abingdon Baptist Church, 2000

HAMMOND, Nigel   *The Book of Abingdon*, Barracuda Books, 1979

HARCOURT, Edward
William (ed.)   *The Harcourt Papers*, James Parker & Co,
c. 1906

HIBBERT,
Christopher (ed.)   *Encyclopaedia of Oxford*, Macmillan, 1988

HILL, J.R. (ed.)   *Oxford Illustrated History of the Royal Navy*,
Oxford University Press, 1995

HOBSON, M.G. (ed.)   *Oxford Council Acts 1752–1801*,
Oxford Historical Society, 1962

HOWARD, John   *The State of the Prisons In England and Wales*,
J. Johnson, C. Dilly, & T. Cadell, 1792

IRELAND, Samuel — *Picturesque Views on the River Thames*, T. & J. Egerton, 1792

LIVERSIDGE, M.J.H. & W.J.H. — *Abingdon Essays*, self-published, 1989

NAYLOR, Leonard G.R. — *The Malthouse of Joseph Tomkins*, self-published, *c.* 1965

PAGE, William (ed.) — *Victoria History of the County of Berkshire* (volume iv), Dawsons, 1972

PRESTON, Arthur E. — *The Church and Parish of St Nicholas Abingdon*, Oxford University Press, 1929

PRESTON, Arthur E. — *The Fairs and Markets of Abingdon* in *Historic Abingdon: Seven Articles* by Preston and Agnes C. Baker, Abbey Press, 1957

RODGER, N.A.M. — *The Wooden World: an anatomy of the Georgian Navy*, Fontana, 1986

SMITH, Jacqueline & CARTER, John — *Inns and Alehouses of Abingdon 1550–1978*, self-published, 1989

THACKER, Fred S. — *The Thames Highway, Volumes I and II*, David & Charles 1968 (first published 1914 and 1920)

THOYTS, Emma E. — *Royal Berkshire Militia*, self-published, 1897

TOWNSEND, James — *A History of Abingdon*, Henry Frowde, 1910

TOWNSEND, James — *News of a Country Town*, Oxford University Press, 1914

TREVELYAN, G.M. — *English Social History*, Reprint Society, 1948

YOUNG, Arthur — *General View of the Agriculture of Oxfordshire*, Augustus M. Kelley, New York, 1969 (first published for the Board of Agriculture and Internal Improvement, 1813)

Index

-+->-<-+-

Index of main names and places, excepting John Castle, David Charteris, Giles Covington, Richard Kilby, and Charles Shury, and excluding all references occurring under the self-named Appendix headings (shown in bold).

A TOWPATH WALK IN OXFORD:

THE CANAL AND RIVER THAMES BETWEEN WOLVERCOTE AND THE CITY

takes the reader on a near-circular seven-mile route along the towpaths of north Oxford. Drawing on archive records and oral histories, *A Towpath Walk In Oxford* describes the notable events and landmarks, and tells the stories of the characters – resourceful, eccentric, or notorious – who have shaped the varied waterway scene that Oxford enjoys today.

BY MARK DAVIES & CATHERINE ROBINSON 2003
(ISBN 0 9535593 1 9)

"A remarkable compendium of historical fact and fiction concerning Oxford's waterways. It is equally readable as a practical walk guide or as a history book."
– CANAL BOAT & INLAND WATERWAYS MAGAZINE

"At times like a pilgrimage, at times like a historical pub crawl ... the perfect combination."
– OXFORD TIMES LIMITED EDITION MAGAZINE

"A most informative text which never loses sight of the human element ... a very easy read despite being choc-full with facts and details."
– CANAL & RIVERBOAT MAGAZINE

"The whole book reads superbly."
– WILLIAM HORWOOD, OXFORD WRITER

"Beautifully done, a model of its kind."
– MARGARET DRABBLE, NOVELIST AND CRITIC

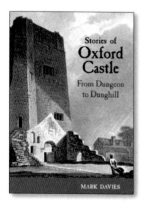

STORIES OF OXFORD CASTLE:

FROM DUNGEON TO DUNGHILL

Stories of Oxford Castle: From Dungeon to Dunghill relates the stories of some of the most daring, devious, or deluded individuals ever to spend time inside the walls of Oxfordshire's county prison.

These stories of imprisonment, transportation, escape, and execution shed new light on the enthralling story of this major Oxford landmark. They also expose in dramatic and often touching detail the social conditions which explain why so many Oxfordshire citizens fell foul of the law in the first place.

BY MARK DAVIES 2006 (ISBN 0 9535593 3 5)

"A comprehensive and gripping account ... a must for anyone interested in Oxford's past."
– OXFORD TIMES

"A fascinating publication."
– FAMILY HISTORY MONTHLY MAGAZINE

"A well-researched history ... most entertaining and informative."
– YOUR FAMILY TREE MAGAZINE

"Essential reading for anyone interested in the history of crime and punishment in the Thames Valley."
– THAMES VIEW MAGAZINE